rise up

dream. plan. hustle. win.

this planner belongs to:

_____

our goals

CAN ONLY BE REACHED
THROUGH A VEHICLE OF A PLAN,
IN WHICH WE MUST **FERVENTLY
BELIEVE**, AND UPON WHICH
WE MUST **VIGOROUSLY ACT**.
THERE IS NO OTHER ROUTE
TO SUCCESS.

———————————————

PABLO PICASSO

2022

july

s	m	t	w	t	f	s
					1	2
3	4	5	6	7	8	9
10	11	12	13	14	15	16
17	18	19	20	21	22	23
24	25	26	27	28	29	30
31						

august

s	m	t	w	t	f	s
	1	2	3	4	5	6
7	8	9	10	11	12	13
14	15	16	17	18	19	20
21	22	23	24	25	26	27
28	29	30	31			

september

s	m	t	w	t	f	s
				1	2	3
4	5	6	7	8	9	10
11	12	13	14	15	16	17
18	19	20	21	22	23	24
25	26	27	28	29	30	

october

s	m	t	w	t	f	s
						1
2	3	4	5	6	7	8
9	10	11	12	13	14	15
16	17	18	19	20	21	22
23	24	25	26	27	28	29
30	31					

november

s	m	t	w	t	f	s
		1	2	3	4	5
6	7	8	9	10	11	12
13	14	15	16	17	18	19
20	21	22	23	24	25	26
27	28	29	30			

december

s	m	t	w	t	f	s
				1	2	3
4	5	6	7	8	9	10
11	12	13	14	15	16	17
18	19	20	21	22	23	24
25	26	27	28	29	30	31

2023

january

s	m	t	w	t	f	s
1	2	3	4	5	6	7
8	9	10	11	12	13	14
15	16	17	18	19	20	21
22	23	24	25	26	27	28
29	30	31				

_____

_____

february

s	m	t	w	t	f	s
			1	2	3	4
5	6	7	8	9	10	11
12	13	14	15	16	17	18
19	20	21	22	23	24	25
26	27	28				

_____

_____

march

s	m	t	w	t	f	s
			1	2	3	4
5	6	7	8	9	10	11
12	13	14	15	16	17	18
19	20	21	22	23	24	25
26	27	28	29	30	31	

_____

_____

april

s	m	t	w	t	f	s
						1
2	3	4	5	6	7	8
9	10	11	12	13	14	15
16	17	18	19	20	21	22
23	24	25	26	27	28	29
30						

_____

_____

may

s	m	t	w	t	f	s
	1	2	3	4	5	6
7	8	9	10	11	12	13
14	15	16	17	18	19	20
21	22	23	24	25	26	27
28	29	30	31			

_____

_____

june

s	m	t	w	t	f	s
				1	2	3
4	5	6	7	8	9	10
11	12	13	14	15	16	17
18	19	20	21	22	23	24
25	26	27	28	29	30	

_____

_____

july

s	m	t	w	t	f	s
						1
2	3	4	5	6	7	8
9	10	11	12	13	14	15
16	17	18	19	20	21	22
23	24	25	26	27	28	29
30	31					

august

s	m	t	w	t	f	s
		1	2	3	4	5
6	7	8	9	10	11	12
13	14	15	16	17	18	19
20	21	22	23	24	25	26
27	28	29	30	31		

september

s	m	t	w	t	f	s
					1	2
3	4	5	6	7	8	9
10	11	12	13	14	15	16
17	18	19	20	21	22	23
24	25	26	27	28	29	30

october

s	m	t	w	t	f	s
1	2	3	4	5	6	7
8	9	10	11	12	13	14
15	16	17	18	19	20	21
22	23	24	25	26	27	28
29	30	31				

november

s	m	t	w	t	f	s
			1	2	3	4
5	6	7	8	9	10	11
12	13	14	15	16	17	18
19	20	21	22	23	24	25
26	27	28	29	30		

december

s	m	t	w	t	f	s
					1	2
3	4	5	6	7	8	9
10	11	12	13	14	15	16
17	18	19	20	21	22	23
24	25	26	27	28	29	30
31						

2024

january

s	m	t	w	t	f	s
	1	2	3	4	5	6
7	8	9	10	11	12	13
14	15	16	17	18	19	20
21	22	23	24	25	26	27
28	29	30	31			

_____

_____

february

s	m	t	w	t	f	s
				1	2	3
4	5	6	7	8	9	10
11	12	13	14	15	16	17
18	19	20	21	22	23	24
25	26	27	28	29		

_____

_____

march

s	m	t	w	t	f	s
					1	2
3	4	5	6	7	8	9
10	11	12	13	14	15	16
17	18	19	20	21	22	23
24	25	26	27	28	29	30
31						

_____

_____

april

s	m	t	w	t	f	s
	1	2	3	4	5	6
7	8	9	10	11	12	13
14	15	16	17	18	19	20
21	22	23	24	25	26	27
28	29	30				

_____

_____

may

s	m	t	w	t	f	s
			1	2	3	4
5	6	7	8	9	10	11
12	13	14	15	16	17	18
19	20	21	22	23	24	25
26	27	28	29	30	31	

_____

_____

june

s	m	t	w	t	f	s
						1
2	3	4	5	6	7	8
9	10	11	12	13	14	15
16	17	18	19	20	21	22
23	24	25	26	27	28	29
30						

_____

_____

july

s	m	t	w	t	f	s
	1	2	3	4	5	6
7	8	9	10	11	12	13
14	15	16	17	18	19	20
21	22	23	24	25	26	27
28	29	30	31			

august

s	m	t	w	t	f	s
				1	2	3
4	5	6	7	8	9	10
11	12	13	14	15	16	17
18	19	20	21	22	23	24
25	26	27	28	29	30	31

september

s	m	t	w	t	f	s
1	2	3	4	5	6	7
8	9	10	11	12	13	14
15	16	17	18	19	20	21
22	23	24	25	26	27	28
29	30					

october

s	m	t	w	t	f	s
		1	2	3	4	5
6	7	8	9	10	11	12
13	14	15	16	17	18	19
20	21	22	23	24	25	26
27	28	29	30	31		

november

s	m	t	w	t	f	s
					1	2
3	4	5	6	7	8	9
10	11	12	13	14	15	16
17	18	19	20	21	22	23
24	25	26	27	28	29	30

december

s	m	t	w	t	f	s
1	2	3	4	5	6	7
8	9	10	11	12	13	14
15	16	17	18	19	20	21
22	23	24	25	26	27	28
29	30	31				

find moira online

@moirakucaba   @moirakucaba   Moira Kucaba

Second Edition

Design by Margaret Cogswell
www.margaretcogswell.com

welcome to your extraordinary life!

I'm Moira Kucaba, and I'll be your guide to the life you know somewhere deep down inside is possible. I'm here to teach, inspire, and equip you with all you need to create the life of your dreams. For starters, let me introduce myself. I was born an entrepreneur. I think being the youngest of six Irish Catholic kids I had to figure a lot of things out by myself and be resourceful. My parents raised me humbly. We didn't have lot of extra money, but we had the important things: love and family.

I remember as a little girl digging through couch cushions to find change, then pedaling my banana seat bike to the canteen at the hospital where my mom worked so I could buy as much candy as my pockets would fit. Then I would sell it back to the neighborhood kids at double the price. When you're the youngest of six, you have to learn how to hustle young. I had many other young entrepreneurial adventures and my parents always said I could do anything I set my mind to.

They gave me belief in myself, and the belief that anything was possible. I believed for a long time that I'd be the first female professional baseball player. There's still time yet. I throw a mean fastball.

From a young age, I wanted to be a doctor. My mom was a nurse but there was always something enticing about being the big wig. I had a fascination with all things medical and a love for helping others so it seemed like a good fit. I had the grades and accolades needed, but my dreams fell by the wayside when I picked up alcohol, and later drugs, and fell into a downward spiral of addiction. By His grace I climbed out of that at 21, only to pick up another addiction: bulimia.

9

My med school dream was in the rearview mirror, but I had a deep-seated desire to fix myself and work in the health field. So, I became a pilates instructor and opened up my first studio when I was 23, because who doesn't move 3,000 miles away to a town where they know no one to open up their own business? Ah, to be young and naive. It has its perks!

I built a thriving business, expanded, and hired more people. After about twelve years, I was bored and decided to sell that business and open a cold-pressed juice company when I was about 35. I had a young family and a dream—to help others on a deeper level, to create something big that really influenced and changed lives. Two and a half years in, I hit rock bottom due to the immense financial and time obligations that running a business requires. My marriage, my kids, my health, my friendships—it was all crumbling. I had crawled out of the shameful pit of bulimia but still struggled with binge eating. As successful as life looked on the outside, the plane was going down in flames.

In 2014, I found a solution. One that literally brought me back to life, physically, mentally, and emotionally. I started an online business and found the tools and the tribe I needed to set me on the road to true success. My husband had his wife back, my kids had their mom back, and I had my fire and myself back. Never in a million years did I think I'd be doing the work I'm doing today, but I can tell you it's more than I could ever have dreamed possible. I'm currently writing this from a first class cabin over the Atlantic. How is this my life?! In 4 years, I built a seven figure business from home and I've had the amazing opportunity to speak to tens of thousands on stages around the country.

I dug in and became obsessed with learning all the tips, tools and tricks for success and compiled them here as your yearly, weekly, and daily guidebook.

This system was born out of necessity. I had figured out the exact path to success but found myself scattered using different planning tools from different sources. It was making me insane! This system brings it all together. This Rise Up Planner teaches you the exact strategies and habits that I created and use to this day to help scale all of my businesses.

This planner is laid out into 2 sections. Each section begins with an overview which will instruct you on how to use that part of the planner. The sections are as follows:

1. A PLANNER to use daily to ensure you are showing up everyday and making it all happen.

2. A tracker for you to jot down your oh-so-important takeaways to HUSTLE on from every podcast, meeting, workshop, and book you read. ALL IN ONE PLACE. Praise baby Jesus!

In addition to this planner, I also created the companion Rise Up: Book of Proof. This is the magic formula to achieving everything you've ever wanted in your life. It's a place to dream your biggest dreams, craft the vision you want for your life, and record your daily wins.

In the Book of Proof, you will learn how to:
• Get crystal clear on the tasks you need to do daily to achieve your goals
• Use "contrasts" + "clarity" statements to achieve the life you deserve
• Adopt a 10 minute morning ritual that sets your soul on fire
• "Future proof" your life and begin to see all you desire come to fruition

Be sure to grab your copy on Amazon!

Welcome to the first day of the rest of your life. The day it all changes, should you so choose! Let's get started!

my top 10 tips for success

*Who you surround yourself with is everything. Find people
that celebrate you when you win and catch you when you fall.*

*Develop a morning routine.
The first hour of the day dictates the remaining 23.*

*Get crystal clear on the life you want to create.
When you focus on the why, the how shows up.*

*Energy is the secret to success. Find the positive in everything, even what
seems negative. There are always blessings. there are always lessons.*

*Learn to master your time. We all have the same 24 hours.
How you spend them will dictate your future.*

*Don't make excuses for your dreams. There are NO excuses when you
really want it. Sacrifice feels better than regret.*

*Lead with a servant's heart. When you expect nothing in return,
you get everything.*

*Judge no one. You probably have no idea how much it's actually shooting
you in the foot. Judgement is all NEGATIVE energy.*

*Compare yourself to no one. It'll not only rob you of your joy,
it'll rob you of your dreams.*

*Reading your vision and write in your Book of Proof daily.
The couple minutes it takes to do this will TRANSFORM your life.*

section 1

DREAM. PLAN.

dream: master your vision

Vision is absolutely everything. If there is one piece of advice I could give you in regards to success, it would be to focus on your vision more than anything else. That's why I created the companion to this planner, The Book Of Proof. It is the number one key to change everything. It's meant to pair perfectly with this planner so that you can get clear on your dreams & vision, and have a plan of action to achieve them. You can purchase it on Amazon.

plan: master your time

My days used to go like this: Get up at 5 am, work my butt off all day ... it's 4pm and I'm wiped out. I look down at my to do list and realized I haven't checked almost anything off. The most important stuff! These were the things I needed to do to make headway and I hadn't done any of them? What in the world had I been doing for the last 11 hours? If you're not clear on what you need to do daily to reach your big end-of-year goals and TRACKING it, your life will slip away with busyness and you won't have much to show for it. Work smarter, not harder.

I've left the weekly "win the week" tracker blank because we all have very different lives, goals, and are at different places in our businesses. These days, my tracker includes things like touch base with my leaders, eat all my greens, date night with hubs, and spend quality time with each child. No matter what, I ALWAYS TRACK Read My Vision, Review Goals, and Book of Proof. The sample Win the Week Tracker is a road map to what you need to do daily to build a successful life.

DO NOT miss out on this step! You can be crystal clear on your vision, your top 3 goals, and even the daily behaviors needed to make it all happen. But executing it is a different story. You have to schedule it into your day, every day. Find the time WHEN you are going to do it and map it out. Some people prefer to schedule their entire week ahead of time and some do best scheduling the night before. I do a little of both.

On Sunday evenings, I chunk down all the things I need to do, schedule in set meetings, future proof my week, and PENCIL in the other things on my tracker. You have WAY more time than you think you do. Something that's often on my list is to have a one-on-one with my leaders. I do all my check ins on the drive home from dropping my kids at school or while sitting in the carpool line for pickup. When you really dissect your time, you will have enough of it, I promise.

Always start with your "ideal week." Block off the times you'd like to do things and then work them around your reality. Review last week. Write in your goals and decide what behaviors you're tracking for the week.

A couple of tips ...
a) Do your least favorite and most impactful actions FIRST. Otherwise they will get pushed to the end of the day and into the next. Ask yourself what activities on your list are the most important in relation to your top 3 goals. Do them FIRST.

b) Don't forget to schedule in NON-WORKING hours. If you are an aspiring entrepreneur, one of the hardest things to create is balance and, let's be real, if you're attempting to build a 6 or 7 figure business, you won't have balance. But you can block out a couple hours each day to detach and be present for your family.

Keep in mind, you won't hit your target every week. Success comes from reattempting and showing up every week. Your success will come from setting your intentions every week, and having a plan even if life does throw it upside down.

master your morning

It's said the first hour of your day determines the next 23. If it wasn't for my morning process, I'd be a certifiable lunatic. No joke. I had this ah-ha several years back. It was Christmas break, the time of year I look forward to most. Yes, I'm that over-the-top person that gets WAY too into Christmas as soon as the turkey is eaten. It was supposed to be magical. I had littles who were excited and I had anticipated it all year.

I found myself at my worst: mommy rage in full tilt. I couldn't control my anger or frustration and I found myself about to strangle my kids. What I realized was, with school being out of session and my schedule shifting, I had let go of my morning time. The 10-30 minutes that grounds me, connects me to God, makes me focus on all I'm grateful for, reminds of of my vision and "pre-paves" the day.

If I go even a few days without it, I'm off kilter. I lose my focus and without focus on the good, all I see is the bad. So let's start easy, shall we?

If you are short on time try on my "3, 3, 3" routine.
3 minutes of gratitude
3 minutes of prayer
3 minutes of visualization (read that VISION!)

Let's break it down ...

Gratitude: It's the magical elixir for life. I don't care how bad you've got it, there is good to see. And trust me, I've been in some really dark places. One of my favorite sayings is, "The universe doesn't hear what you say, it hears what you feel." So the point of this is to "feel" your way into it. Start with anything: I'm grateful for my home, my kids' school, my kids' teachers, the influences in their lives, name certain people, get the momentum going and let it roll. You'll soon find yourself smiling.

Prayer: Don't get scared about this one if you're not a big believer in the God thing. Pray for those you love. Ask a power greater than you to work through you.

Ask to be a vessel. To serve. When you wake up every day with a servant's heart, success with everything–relationships, business, etc.–will come.

One of my favorite simple prayers is… "God, take me where you want me to go, let me meet who you want me to meet, tell me what you want me to say, and keep me out of your way." That didn't even take 3 minutes. Ha!

Visualization: I'm a HUGE believer in this! What I do most mornings is I pre-pave my day. I see the day happening and I see myself showing up as my best. I think about the hiccups I may run into and instead I see them working out beautifully. I see myself waking up my kids, driving them to school laughing, coming home and rocking my business, greeting my husband with a kiss, crushing my workout, and going to bed with a smile on my face.

So, now you've pre-paved the day. Let's take a look at the bigger vision for your life, where you'll be in just 2-3 years. Take out that vision you wrote and read it. FEEL it. Get excited about where you are going. Remember when you focus on the WHY, the HOW will show up.

About 10 years ago I was studying meditation with a guru and waking up every day to med- itate. After several years (although the practice was impacting my life) I never found myself eager to get out of bed. I finally decided to wake up and listen to some guided teachings and meditations on Youtube and found myself instantly invigorated and excited about my morning process. I've compiled some of my favorites into a playlist, which you find by searching for Moira Kucaba on YouTube.

Your morning routine has to energize and invigorate you. If it doesn't, change it up and COMMIT to the new process.

Trust me, your morning routine is the key to it all.

> "Rise at 5am. Spend the first hour on fitness, gratitude and reading. The way you start your day drives how beautifully you live it."
> *Robin Sharma*

master your energy

Let's chat exercise, nutrition, and sleep. All are key factors in a successful life. I'm a big fan of working out first thing in the morning. Think about it: when you wake up and do something hard, push yourself physically, you are setting the foundation for your day. You can do hard things! You've proven it to yourself in the first hour! And if it's more gentle exercise? Great! You've woken up your body, gotten your blood flowing and are feeling self love and confidence in doing something for yourself first thing. You can't pour from an empty cup. Fill yours first.

I struggled with disordered eating for over 20 years. It was more painful and harder to overcome than my alcohol and drug addictions. After all, we can't abstain from food, right? I finally found a solution when I started to care more about how I felt than how I looked. You can't be clear-minded, energetic, joyful, and, I believe, be in the flow of success when you are feeding your body crap. Try to eat real food, foods packed with nutrients that give you life. You truly are what you eat and when I'm eating a bunch of sugary, high fat foods, it alters my mind to a negative one.

Ah sleep ... I'm still working on this one a bit. I have a lot of team calls at night which really energize me and then I have a hard time sleeping. But I've learned to prioritize it. Without sleep, we are foggy and SO much less productive.

Now that we've covered the basics—exercise, nutrition and sleep—I need to point out that your energy comes almost entirely from your mind. Sounds crazy, huh? Let's put it to the test!

Have you ever had little to no sleep and had more energy than you could ever imagine? So, sleep is important but not entirely the answer. Food, you may guess? Important too, but how do you feel after Thanksgiving? Full of energy? I think not. Your thoughts and your story about every circumstance in your life have more power than anything to energize you!

Let me give you two powerful prompts you can hold in your mind that have the power to change everything in your life. Yes, I'm serious. Everything. No matter what life throws at you, a flat tire, a traffic jam, a scathing judgement, a death, illness, addiction (yes I've gone through them all), these key phrases will change everything.

1. LIFE IS HAPPENING FOR YOU.
Be careful of the stories you make up in your mind and never, ever play the victim. This one sentence will turn everything on its head and prompt you to start looking for the lesson and not end up in the downward spiral of thoughts and events that haven't even occurred yet. Every tragedy and so-called failure I've gone through has made me a better person, guided me to the next right decision, taught me so much, and no matter how dark the event, I see the blessing and how in fact it was ALL HAPPENING FOR ME.

2. WHAT AM I EXCITED ABOUT TODAY?
I used to find myself hitting the ground running with my to-do list everyday. It would go something like this, " I have to meditate, workout, get the kids off to school, pack for a trip, lead a team call, check in with my clients, clean the house, take care of the dog, get to a meeting ..." The list went on and on. I would see it all as a "have to." UGH! And I'd be totally drained just THINKING about what I had to do, not "get" to do. I simply started asking myself that one simple question, "What am I excited about?" And everything shifted from a check on my list, to a gift.

We have the choice everyday to see the big things and the small things as gifts. Almost all of us are beyond blessed if we choose to see it. What we focus on expands. Choose to see the good.

(The next few pages show a sample of what an ideal week and month might look like...)

dream. plan. hustle. win.

monthly goals & intentions

family/home
quality time with kids after school

relationships
date night every Thurs.

my body
eat all my veggies, lose 2 lbs.

finances
1k/month

business
10 new customers, 4 new team members, Insta training, Go live 3 days a week on Facebook, attend 1 webinar

fun/community
volunteer at children's hospital

personal development I'm committed to
read The Go-Giver by Bob Berg

business development I'm committed to
Instagram training

time to reflect

biggest accomplishments last month?
Ran my first 5K!!!

Saved $1,500

areas I need to improve this month?
Write in my book of Proof daily!

Be more consistent on social media

High Vibe Habit Stacker

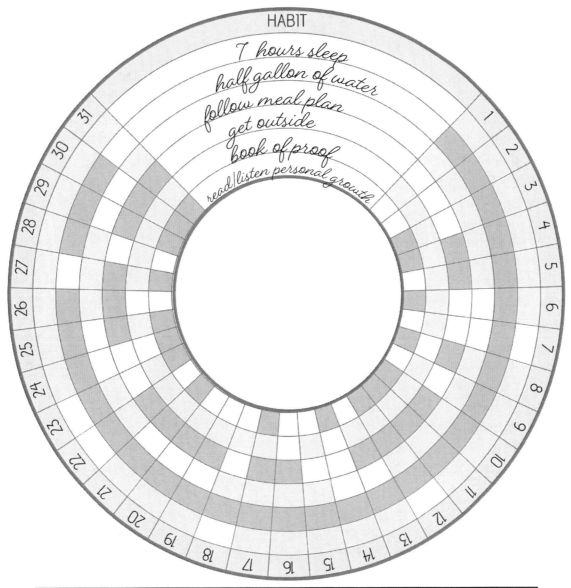

Habit Stack	Days Complete	Percentage Complete
7 hours sleep	26	84%
half gallon of water	29	94%
follow meal plan	20	65%
get outside	19	61%
book of proof	26	84%
read/listen personal development	17	55%

sample week

review last week/ plan this week ☑

top three yearly goals
1. TOP 100
2. Save 15k
3. Complete half marathon

top three monthly goals
1. 10 new customers
2. 4 new team members
3. Finish Instagram training

top three weekly goals
1. 4 new customers
2. 1 new team member
3. Instagram training

three most important meetings/events
1. Coffee w/ Julia
2. Date night
3. Mastermind call

	monday		tuesday	
6	morning process, workout		morning process, workout	
7				
8	team check in		team check in	
9	FOCUS HOUR		FOCUS HOUR	
10				
11			corporate training call	
12				
1				
2				
3	family time		family time	
4	family time		family time	
5	family time		family time	
6	family time		family time	
7	family time		family time	
8	first 30 call			
9	team call			
10				
invites	business	customer	business	customer

win the week

Action	Mon	Tues	Weds	Thurs	Fri	Sat	Sun	Goal	Actual	%
Read Vision/Review Goals	✓	✓	✓	✓		✓	✓	7	6	85
Book of Proof	✓	✓	✓		✓	✓	✓	7	6	85
Workout	✓	✓	✓	✓	✓	✓	✓	7	7	100
Personal Development	✓	✓		✓	✓	✓		7	5	71
Add Followers	✓	✓	✓	✓	✓	x	x	5	5	100
Post Social Media	✓	✓	✓	✓	✓		✓	7	6	85
5-7 Stories	✓	✓	✓	✓	✓	✓	✓	7	7	100
Respond to new notifications	✓	✓		✓	✓	x	x	5	4	80
Invite (5, ⑩, 25)	**10**	**10**	**10**	**9**	**11**	x	x	50	50	100
Follow Ups	✓	✓	✓	✓		x	x	5	4	80
Send Thank You's	✓	✓	✓	✓	✓	✓	✓	7	7	100

wednesday	thursday	friday	saturday	sunday	
morning process, workout	morning process, workout	morning process, workout			6
	recognition day				7
team check in	team check in	team check in			8
FOCUS HOUR	FOCUS HOUR	FOCUS HOUR			9
			hip hop practice		10
		dentist appt.		meal plan	11
				grocery store	12
	mastermind call	lunch with hubs			1
			birthday party		2
family time	family time	family time		meal prep	3
family time	family time	family time			4
family time	family time	family time		review/plan week	5
baseball game	family time	baseball game			6
family time	family time	family time			7
			Topka's for dinner	new team member call	8
				push call	9
					10
business	customer	business	customer	business	customer	business	customer	business	customer

marketing plan

monday	tuesday	wednesday	thursday	friday	saturday	sunday
call to action	motivation monday	ask for referrals	go live on social media	post on business page	share personal journey	live event

remember, life happens for you, not to you.

WINS _helped 2 new people, great date night_

LOSSES _didn't hit invite goal_

HOW CAN I IMPROVE? _schedule my time better_

Month:

dream. plan. hustle. win.

monthly goals & intentions

| family/home | relationships |

| my body | finances |

| business | fun/community |

| personal development I'm committed to | business development I'm committed to |

time to reflect

biggest accomplishments
last month?

areas I need to improve
this month?

_____

_____

_____

_____

High Vibe Habit Stacker

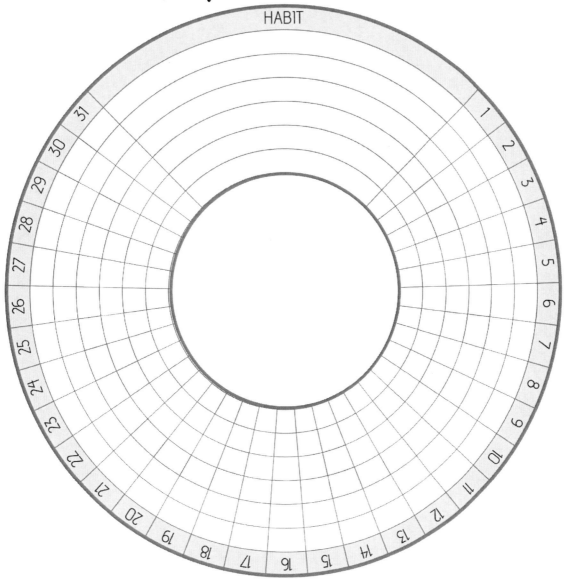

HABIT

Habit Stack	Days Complete	Percentage Complete
		%
		%
		%
		%
		%
		%

Month:

_____

Notes:

_____

_____

_____

_____

_____

_____

_____

_____

_____

_____

sunday	monday	tuesday

wednesday	thursday	friday	saturday

weekly to-do's

- [ ] _____
- [ ] _____
- [ ] _____
- [ ] _____
- [ ] _____
- [ ] _____
- [ ] _____
- [ ] _____
- [ ] _____
- [ ] _____
- [ ] _____
- [ ] _____
- [ ] _____
- [ ] _____
- [ ] _____
- [ ] _____
- [ ] _____

- [ ] _____
- [ ] _____
- [ ] _____
- [ ] _____
- [ ] _____
- [ ] _____
- [ ] _____
- [ ] _____
- [ ] _____
- [ ] _____
- [ ] _____
- [ ] _____
- [ ] _____
- [ ] _____
- [ ] _____
- [ ] _____
- [ ] _____

weekly to-do's

- [ ] _____
- [ ] _____
- [ ] _____
- [ ] _____
- [ ] _____
- [ ] _____
- [ ] _____
- [ ] _____
- [ ] _____
- [ ] _____
- [ ] _____
- [ ] _____
- [ ] _____
- [ ] _____
- [ ] _____
- [ ] _____
- [ ] _____
- [ ] _____

- [ ] _____
- [ ] _____
- [ ] _____
- [ ] _____
- [ ] _____
- [ ] _____
- [ ] _____
- [ ] _____
- [ ] _____
- [ ] _____
- [ ] _____
- [ ] _____
- [ ] _____
- [ ] _____
- [ ] _____
- [ ] _____
- [ ] _____
- [ ] _____

monthly enrollments

Date	Name						

business goals

of new customers

goal _____

actual _____

○ ○ ○ ○ ○
○ ○ ○ ○ ○
○ ○ ○ ○ ○
○ ○ ○ ○ ○

of new team members

goal _____

actual _____

○ ○ ○ ○ ○
○ ○ ○ ○ ○
○ ○ ○ ○ ○
○ ○ ○ ○ ○

of team advancements

goal _____

actual _____

○ ○ ○ ○ ○
○ ○ ○ ○ ○
○ ○ ○ ○ ○
○ ○ ○ ○ ○

of customer invites

goal _____

actual _____

of business opportunity invites

goal _____

actual _____

notes

customer hot list

1.
2.
3.
4.
5.
6.
7.
8.
9.
10.
11.
12.
13.
14.
15.
16.
17.
18.
19.
20.

21.
22.
23.
24.
25.
26.
27.
28.
29.
30.
31.
32.
33.
34.
35.
36.
37.
38.
39.
40.

business hot list

1.
2.
3.
4.
5.
6.
7.
8.
9.
10.
11.
12.
13.
14.
15.
16.
17.
18.
19.
20.

21.
22.
23.
24.
25.
26.
27.
28.
29.
30.
31.
32.
33.
34.
35.
36.
37.
38.
39.
40.

week of: _____

top three yearly goals
1.
2.
3.

top three monthly goals
1.
2.
3.

top three weekly goals
1.
2.
3.

three most important
meetings/events
1.
2.
3.

	monday		tuesday	
6				
7				
8				
9				
10				
11				
12				
1				
2				
3				
4				
5				
6				
7				
8				
9				
10				
invites	business	customer	business	customer

win the week

Action	Mon	Tues	Weds	Thurs	Fri	Sat	Sun	Goal	Actual	%
Read Vision/Review Goals										
Book of Proof										

wednesday		thursday		friday		saturday		sunday		
										6
										7
										8
										9
										10
										11
										12
										1
										2
										3
										4
										5
										6
										7
										8
										9
										10
business	customer	business	customer	business	customer	business	customer	business	customer	

marketing plan

monday	tuesday	wednesday	thursday	friday	saturday	sunday

remember, life happens for you, not to you.

WINS _____

LOSSES _____

HOW CAN I IMPROVE? _____

week of: _____

top three yearly goals
1.
2.
3.

top three monthly goals
1.
2.
3.

top three weekly goals
1.
2.
3.

three most important
meetings/events
1.
2.
3.

	monday		tuesday	
6				
7				
8				
9				
10				
11				
12				
1				
2				
3				
4				
5				
6				
7				
8				
9				
10				
invites	business	customer	business	customer

win the week

Action	Mon	Tues	Weds	Thurs	Fri	Sat	Sun	Goal	Actual	%
Read Vision/Review Goals										
Book of Proof										

wednesday	thursday	friday	saturday	sunday	
					6
					7
					8
					9
					10
					11
					12
					1
					2
					3
					4
					5
					6
					7
					8
					9
					10

business	customer	business	customer	business	customer	business	customer	business	customer

marketing plan

monday	tuesday	wednesday	thursday	friday	saturday	sunday

remember, life happens for you, not to you.

WINS _____

LOSSES _____

HOW CAN I IMPROVE? _____

week of: _____

review last week/ plan this week	☐

top three yearly goals
1.
2.
3.

top three monthly goals
1.
2.
3.

top three weekly goals
1.
2.
3.

three most important
meetings/events
1.
2.
3.

	monday		tuesday	
6				
7				
8				
9				
10				
11				
12				
1				
2				
3				
4				
5				
6				
7				
8				
9				
10				
invites	business	customer	business	customer

win the week

Action	Mon	Tues	Weds	Thurs	Fri	Sat	Sun	Goal	Actual	%
Read Vision/Review Goals										
Book of Proof										

wednesday	thursday	friday	saturday	sunday	
					6
					7
					8
					9
					10
					11
					12
					1
					2
					3
					4
					5
					6
					7
					8
					9
					10

business	customer	business	customer	business	customer	business	customer	business	customer

marketing plan

monday	tuesday	wednesday	thursday	friday	saturday	sunday

remember, life happens for you, not to you.

WINS _____

LOSSES _____

HOW CAN I IMPROVE? _____

week of: _____

top three yearly goals
1.
2.
3.

top three monthly goals
1.
2.
3.

top three weekly goals
1.
2.
3.

three most important
meetings/events
1.
2.
3.

	monday		tuesday	
6				
7				
8				
9				
10				
11				
12				
1				
2				
3				
4				
5				
6				
7				
8				
9				
10				
invites	business	customer	business	customer

win the week

Action	Mon	Tues	Weds	Thurs	Fri	Sat	Sun	Goal	Actual	%
Read Vision/Review Goals										
Book of Proof										

wednesday		thursday		friday		saturday		sunday		
										6
										7
										8
										9
										10
										11
										12
										1
										2
										3
										4
										5
										6
										7
										8
										9
										10
business	customer	business	customer	business	customer	business	customer	business	customer	

marketing plan

monday	tuesday	wednesday	thursday	friday	saturday	sunday

remember, life happens for you, not to you.

WINS _____

LOSSES _____

HOW CAN I IMPROVE? _____

week of: _____

review last week/
plan this week ☐

top three yearly goals
1.
2.
3.

top three monthly goals
1.
2.
3.

top three weekly goals
1.
2.
3.

three most important
meetings/events
1.
2.
3.

	monday		tuesday	
6				
7				
8				
9				
10				
11				
12				
1				
2				
3				
4				
5				
6				
7				
8				
9				
10				
invites	business	customer	business	customer

win the week

Action	Mon	Tues	Weds	Thurs	Fri	Sat	Sun	Goal	Actual	%
Read Vision/Review Goals										
Book of Proof										

wednesday		thursday		friday		saturday		sunday		
										6
										7
										8
										9
										10
										11
										12
										1
										2
										3
										4
										5
										6
										7
										8
										9
										10
business	customer	business	customer	business	customer	business	customer	business	customer	

marketing plan

monday	tuesday	wednesday	thursday	friday	saturday	sunday

remember, life happens for you, not to you.

WINS _____

LOSSES _____

HOW CAN I IMPROVE? _____

Month:

dream. plan. hustle. win.

monthly goals & intentions

family/home

relationships

my body

finances

business

fun/community

personal development I'm committed to

business development I'm committed to

time to reflect

biggest accomplishments
last month?

areas I need to improve
this month?

_____

_____

_____

_____

High Vibe Habit Stacker

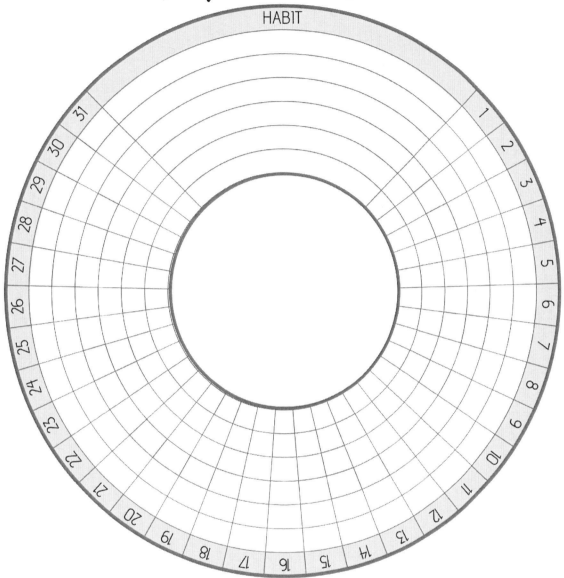

HABIT

Habit Stack	Days Complete	Percentage Complete
		%
		%
		%
		%
		%
		%

Month:

_____

Notes:

_____
_____
_____
_____
_____
_____
_____
_____
_____
_____

sunday	monday	tuesday

wednesday	thursday	friday	saturday

weekly to-do's

- [ ] _____
- [ ] _____
- [ ] _____
- [ ] _____
- [ ] _____
- [ ] _____
- [ ] _____
- [ ] _____
- [ ] _____
- [ ] _____
- [ ] _____
- [ ] _____
- [ ] _____
- [ ] _____
- [ ] _____
- [ ] _____
- [ ] _____
- [ ] _____

- [ ] _____
- [ ] _____
- [ ] _____
- [ ] _____
- [ ] _____
- [ ] _____
- [ ] _____
- [ ] _____
- [ ] _____
- [ ] _____
- [ ] _____
- [ ] _____
- [ ] _____
- [ ] _____
- [ ] _____
- [ ] _____
- [ ] _____
- [ ] _____

weekly to-do's

- [ ] _____
- [ ] _____
- [ ] _____
- [ ] _____
- [ ] _____
- [ ] _____
- [ ] _____
- [ ] _____
- [ ] _____
- [ ] _____
- [ ] _____
- [ ] _____
- [ ] _____
- [ ] _____
- [ ] _____
- [ ] _____
- [ ] _____
- [ ] _____

- [ ] _____
- [ ] _____
- [ ] _____
- [ ] _____
- [ ] _____
- [ ] _____
- [ ] _____
- [ ] _____
- [ ] _____
- [ ] _____
- [ ] _____
- [ ] _____
- [ ] _____
- [ ] _____
- [ ] _____
- [ ] _____
- [ ] _____
- [ ] _____

monthly enrollments

Date	Name						

business goals

of new customers

goal _____

actual _____

○ ○ ○ ○ ○
○ ○ ○ ○ ○
○ ○ ○ ○ ○
○ ○ ○ ○ ○

of new team members

goal _____

actual _____

○ ○ ○ ○ ○
○ ○ ○ ○ ○
○ ○ ○ ○ ○
○ ○ ○ ○ ○

of team advancements

goal _____

actual _____

○ ○ ○ ○ ○
○ ○ ○ ○ ○
○ ○ ○ ○ ○
○ ○ ○ ○ ○

of customer invites

goal _____

actual _____

# of business opportunity invites

goal _____

actual _____

notes

customer hot list

1.	21.
2.	22.
3.	23.
4.	24.
5.	25.
6.	26.
7.	27.
8.	28.
9.	29.
10.	30.
11.	31.
12.	32.
13.	33.
14.	34.
15.	35.
16.	36.
17.	37.
18.	38.
19.	39.
20.	40.

business hot list

1.

2.

3.

4.

5.

6.

7.

8.

9.

10.

11.

12.

13.

14.

15.

16.

17.

18.

19.

20.

21.

22.

23.

24.

25.

26.

27.

28.

29.

30.

31.

32.

33.

34.

35.

36.

37.

38.

39.

40.

week of: _____

| review last week/ plan this week | ☐ |

top three yearly goals
1.
2.
3.

top three monthly goals
1.
2.
3.

top three weekly goals
1.
2.
3.

three most important
meetings/events
1.
2.
3.

	monday ☐		tuesday ☐	
6				
7				
8				
9				
10				
11				
12				
1				
2				
3				
4				
5				
6				
7				
8				
9				
10				
invites	business	customer	business	customer

win the week

Action	Mon	Tues	Weds	Thurs	Fri	Sat	Sun	Goal	Actual	%
Read Vision/Review Goals										
Book of Proof										

wednesday		thursday		friday		saturday		sunday		
										6
										7
										8
										9
										10
										11
										12
										1
										2
										3
										4
										5
										6
										7
										8
										9
										10
business	customer	business	customer	business	customer	business	customer	business	customer	

marketing plan

monday	tuesday	wednesday	thursday	friday	saturday	sunday

remember, life happens for you, not to you.

WINS _____

LOSSES _____

HOW CAN I IMPROVE? _____

week of: _____

<table>
<tr><td>review last week/
plan this week</td><td>☐</td></tr>
</table>

top three yearly goals
1.
2.
3.

top three monthly goals
1.
2.
3.

top three weekly goals
1.
2.
3.

three most important
meetings/events
1.
2.
3.

	monday ☐		tuesday ☐	
6				
7				
8				
9				
10				
11				
12				
1				
2				
3				
4				
5				
6				
7				
8				
9				
10				
invites	business	customer	business	customer

win the week

Action	Mon	Tues	Weds	Thurs	Fri	Sat	Sun	Goal	Actual	%
Read Vision/Review Goals										
Book of Proof										

wednesday		thursday		friday		saturday		sunday		
										6
										7
										8
										9
										10
										11
										12
										1
										2
										3
										4
										5
										6
										7
										8
										9
										10
business	customer	business	customer	business	customer	business	customer	business	customer	

marketing plan

monday	tuesday	wednesday	thursday	friday	saturday	sunday

remember, life happens for you, not to you.

WINS _____

LOSSES _____

HOW CAN I IMPROVE? _____

week of: _____

review last week/
plan this week ☐

top three yearly goals
1.
2.
3.

top three monthly goals
1.
2.
3.

top three weekly goals
1.
2.
3.

three most important
meetings/events
1.
2.
3.

	monday		tuesday	
6				
7				
8				
9				
10				
11				
12				
1				
2				
3				
4				
5				
6				
7				
8				
9				
10				
invites	business	customer	business	customer

win the week

Action	Mon	Tues	Weds	Thurs	Fri	Sat	Sun	Goal	Actual	%
Read Vision/Review Goals										
Book of Proof										

wednesday		thursday		friday		saturday		sunday		
										6
										7
										8
										9
										10
										11
										12
										1
										2
										3
										4
										5
										6
										7
										8
										9
										10
business	customer	business	customer	business	customer	business	customer	business	customer	

marketing plan

monday	tuesday	wednesday	thursday	friday	saturday	sunday

remember, life happens for you, not to you.

WINS _____

LOSSES _____

HOW CAN I IMPROVE? _____

week of: _____

top three yearly goals
1.
2.
3.

top three monthly goals
1.
2.
3.

top three weekly goals
1.
2.
3.

three most important
meetings/events
1.
2.
3.

	monday		tuesday	
6				
7				
8				
9				
10				
11				
12				
1				
2				
3				
4				
5				
6				
7				
8				
9				
10				
invites	business	customer	business	customer

win the week

Action	Mon	Tues	Weds	Thurs	Fri	Sat	Sun	Goal	Actual	%
Read Vision/Review Goals										
Book of Proof										

wednesday		thursday		friday		saturday		sunday		
										6
										7
										8
										9
										10
										11
										12
										1
										2
										3
										4
										5
										6
										7
										8
										9
										10
business	customer	business	customer	business	customer	business	customer	business	customer	

marketing plan

monday	tuesday	wednesday	thursday	friday	saturday	sunday

remember, life happens for you, not to you.

WINS _____

LOSSES _____

HOW CAN I IMPROVE? _____

week of: _____

top three yearly goals
1.
2.
3.

top three monthly goals
1.
2.
3.

top three weekly goals
1.
2.
3.

three most important
meetings/events
1.
2.
3.

	monday		tuesday	
6				
7				
8				
9				
10				
11				
12				
1				
2				
3				
4				
5				
6				
7				
8				
9				
10				
invites	business	customer	business	customer

win the week

Action	Mon	Tues	Weds	Thurs	Fri	Sat	Sun	Goal	Actual	%
Read Vision/Review Goals										
Book of Proof										

wednesday		thursday		friday		saturday		sunday		
										6
										7
										8
										9
										10
										11
										12
										1
										2
										3
										4
										5
										6
										7
										8
										9
										10
business	customer	business	customer	business	customer	business	customer	business	customer	

marketing plan

monday	tuesday	wednesday	thursday	friday	saturday	sunday

remember, life happens for you, not to you.

WINS _____

LOSSES _____

HOW CAN I IMPROVE? _____

Month:

dream. plan. hustle. win.

monthly goals & intentions

family/home

relationships

my body

finances

business

fun/community

personal development I'm committed to

business development I'm committed to

time to reflect

biggest accomplishments
last month?

areas I need to improve
this month?

_____

_____

_____

_____

High Vibe Habit Stacker

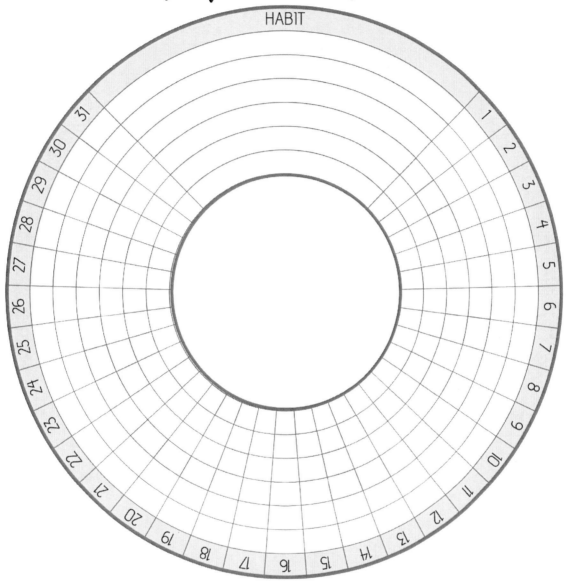

HABIT

Habit Stack	Days Complete	Percentage Complete
		%
		%
		%
		%
		%
		%

Month:

_____

Notes:

_____

_____

_____

_____

_____

_____

_____

_____

_____

_____

sunday	monday	tuesday

wednesday	thursday	friday	saturday

weekly to-do's

- [ ] _____
- [ ] _____
- [ ] _____
- [ ] _____
- [ ] _____
- [ ] _____
- [ ] _____
- [ ] _____
- [ ] _____
- [ ] _____
- [ ] _____
- [ ] _____
- [ ] _____
- [ ] _____
- [ ] _____
- [ ] _____
- [ ] _____

- [ ] _____
- [ ] _____
- [ ] _____
- [ ] _____
- [ ] _____
- [ ] _____
- [ ] _____
- [ ] _____
- [ ] _____
- [ ] _____
- [ ] _____
- [ ] _____
- [ ] _____
- [ ] _____
- [ ] _____
- [ ] _____
- [ ] _____

weekly to-do's

- [ ] _____
- [ ] _____
- [ ] _____
- [ ] _____
- [ ] _____
- [ ] _____
- [ ] _____
- [ ] _____
- [ ] _____
- [ ] _____
- [ ] _____
- [ ] _____
- [ ] _____
- [ ] _____
- [ ] _____
- [ ] _____
- [ ] _____

- [ ] _____
- [ ] _____
- [ ] _____
- [ ] _____
- [ ] _____
- [ ] _____
- [ ] _____
- [ ] _____
- [ ] _____
- [ ] _____
- [ ] _____
- [ ] _____
- [ ] _____
- [ ] _____
- [ ] _____
- [ ] _____
- [ ] _____

monthly enrollments

Date	Name						

business goals

of new customers

goal _____

actual _____

○ ○ ○ ○ ○
○ ○ ○ ○ ○
○ ○ ○ ○ ○
○ ○ ○ ○ ○

of new team members

goal _____

actual _____

○ ○ ○ ○ ○
○ ○ ○ ○ ○
○ ○ ○ ○ ○
○ ○ ○ ○ ○

of team advancements

goal _____

actual _____

○ ○ ○ ○ ○
○ ○ ○ ○ ○
○ ○ ○ ○ ○
○ ○ ○ ○ ○

of customer invites

goal _____

actual _____

of business opportunity invites

goal _____

actual _____

notes

customer hot list

1.	21.
2.	22.
3.	23.
4.	24.
5.	25.
6.	26.
7.	27.
8.	28.
9.	29.
10.	30.
11.	31.
12.	32.
13.	33.
14.	34.
15.	35.
16.	36.
17.	37.
18.	38.
19.	39.
20.	40.

business hot list

1.

2.

3.

4.

5.

6.

7.

8.

9.

10.

11.

12.

13.

14.

15.

16.

17.

18.

19.

20.

21.

22.

23.

24.

25.

26.

27.

28.

29.

30.

31.

32.

33.

34.

35.

36.

37.

38.

39.

40.

week of: _____

review last week/ plan this week	☐

top three yearly goals
1.
2.
3.

top three monthly goals
1.
2.
3.

top three weekly goals
1.
2.
3.

three most important meetings/events
1.
2.
3.

	monday		tuesday	
6				
7				
8				
9				
10				
11				
12				
1				
2				
3				
4				
5				
6				
7				
8				
9				
10				
invites	business	customer	business	customer

win the week

Action	Mon	Tues	Weds	Thurs	Fri	Sat	Sun	Goal	Actual	%
Read Vision/Review Goals										
Book of Proof										

wednesday		thursday		friday		saturday		sunday		
										6
										7
										8
										9
										10
										11
										12
										1
										2
										3
										4
										5
										6
										7
										8
										9
										10
business	customer	business	customer	business	customer	business	customer	business	customer	

marketing plan

monday	tuesday	wednesday	thursday	friday	saturday	sunday

remember, life happens for you, not to you.

WINS _____

LOSSES _____

HOW CAN I IMPROVE? _____

week of: _____

review last week/ plan this week	☐

top three yearly goals
1.
2.
3.

top three monthly goals
1.
2.
3.

top three weekly goals
1.
2.
3.

three most important
meetings/events
1.
2.
3.

	monday		tuesday	
6				
7				
8				
9				
10				
11				
12				
1				
2				
3				
4				
5				
6				
7				
8				
9				
10				
invites	business	customer	business	customer

win the week

Action	Mon	Tues	Weds	Thurs	Fri	Sat	Sun	Goal	Actual	%
Read Vision/Review Goals										
Book of Proof										

wednesday		thursday		friday		saturday		sunday		
										6
										7
										8
										9
										10
										11
										12
										1
										2
										3
										4
										5
										6
										7
										8
										9
										10
business	customer	business	customer	business	customer	business	customer	business	customer	

marketing plan

monday	tuesday	wednesday	thursday	friday	saturday	sunday

remember, life happens for you, not to you.

WINS _____

LOSSES _____

HOW CAN I IMPROVE? _____

week of: _____

review last week/
plan this week ☐

top three yearly goals
1.
2.
3.

top three monthly goals
1.
2.
3.

top three weekly goals
1.
2.
3.

three most important
meetings/events
1.
2.
3.

	monday		tuesday	
6				
7				
8				
9				
10				
11				
12				
1				
2				
3				
4				
5				
6				
7				
8				
9				
10				
invites	business	customer	business	customer

win the week

Action	Mon	Tues	Weds	Thurs	Fri	Sat	Sun	Goal	Actual	%
Read Vision/Review Goals										
Book of Proof										

wednesday		thursday		friday		saturday		sunday		
										6
										7
										8
										9
										10
										11
										12
										1
										2
										3
										4
										5
										6
										7
										8
										9
										10
business	customer	business	customer	business	customer	business	customer	business	customer	

marketing plan

monday	tuesday	wednesday	thursday	friday	saturday	sunday

remember, life happens for you, not to you.

WINS _____

LOSSES _____

HOW CAN I IMPROVE? _____

week of: _____

review last week/ plan this week ☐

top three yearly goals
1.
2.
3.

top three monthly goals
1.
2.
3.

top three weekly goals
1.
2.
3.

three most important meetings/events
1.
2.
3.

	monday		tuesday	
6				
7				
8				
9				
10				
11				
12				
1				
2				
3				
4				
5				
6				
7				
8				
9				
10				
invites	business	customer	business	customer

win the week

Action	Mon	Tues	Weds	Thurs	Fri	Sat	Sun	Goal	Actual	%
Read Vision/Review Goals										
Book of Proof										

wednesday		thursday		friday		saturday		sunday		
										6
										7
										8
										9
										10
										11
										12
										1
										2
										3
										4
										5
										6
										7
										8
										9
										10
business	customer	business	customer	business	customer	business	customer	business	customer	

marketing plan

monday	tuesday	wednesday	thursday	friday	saturday	sunday

remember, life happens for you, not to you.

WINS _____

LOSSES _____

HOW CAN I IMPROVE? _____

week of: _____

	monday		tuesday	
6				
7				
8				
9				
10				
11				
12				
1				
2				
3				
4				
5				
6				
7				
8				
9				
10				
invites	business	customer	business	customer

review last week/
plan this week ☐

top three yearly goals
1.
2.
3.

top three monthly goals
1.
2.
3.

top three weekly goals
1.
2.
3.

three most important
meetings/events
1.
2.
3.

win the week

Action	Mon	Tues	Weds	Thurs	Fri	Sat	Sun	Goal	Actual	%
Read Vision/Review Goals										
Book of Proof										

wednesday		thursday		friday		saturday		sunday		
										6
										7
										8
										9
										10
										11
										12
										1
										2
										3
										4
										5
										6
										7
										8
										9
										10
business	customer	business	customer	business	customer	business	customer	business	customer	

marketing plan

monday	tuesday	wednesday	thursday	friday	saturday	sunday

remember, life happens for you, not to you.

WINS _____

LOSSES _____

HOW CAN I IMPROVE? _____

Month:

dream. plan. hustle. win.

monthly goals & intentions

family/home

relationships

my body

finances

business

fun/community

personal development I'm committed to

business development I'm committed to

time to reflect

biggest accomplishments
last month?

areas I need to improve
this month?

_____

_____

_____

_____

High Vibe Habit Stacker

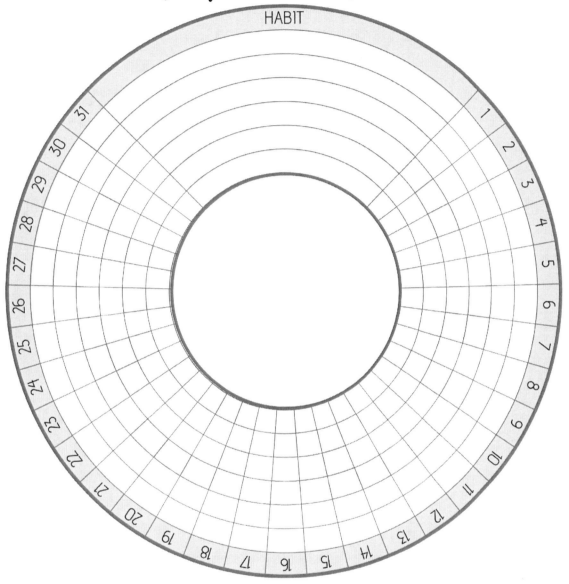

Habit Stack	Days Complete	Percentage Complete
		%
		%
		%
		%
		%
		%

Month:

_____

Notes:

_____

_____

_____

_____

_____

_____

_____

_____

_____

_____

sunday	monday	tuesday

wednesday	thursday	friday	saturday

weekly to-do's

☐ _____
☐ _____
☐ _____
☐ _____
☐ _____
☐ _____
☐ _____
☐ _____
☐ _____
☐ _____
☐ _____
☐ _____
☐ _____
☐ _____
☐ _____
☐ _____
☐ _____

☐ _____
☐ _____
☐ _____
☐ _____
☐ _____
☐ _____
☐ _____
☐ _____
☐ _____
☐ _____
☐ _____
☐ _____
☐ _____
☐ _____
☐ _____
☐ _____
☐ _____

weekly to-do's

- [ ] _____
- [ ] _____
- [ ] _____
- [ ] _____
- [ ] _____
- [ ] _____
- [ ] _____
- [ ] _____
- [ ] _____
- [ ] _____
- [ ] _____
- [ ] _____
- [ ] _____
- [ ] _____
- [ ] _____
- [ ] _____
- [ ] _____

- [ ] _____
- [ ] _____
- [ ] _____
- [ ] _____
- [ ] _____
- [ ] _____
- [ ] _____
- [ ] _____
- [ ] _____
- [ ] _____
- [ ] _____
- [ ] _____
- [ ] _____
- [ ] _____
- [ ] _____
- [ ] _____
- [ ] _____

monthly enrollments

Date	Name						

business goals

of new customers

goal _____

actual _____

○ ○ ○ ○ ○
○ ○ ○ ○ ○
○ ○ ○ ○ ○
○ ○ ○ ○ ○

of new team members

goal _____

actual _____

○ ○ ○ ○ ○
○ ○ ○ ○ ○
○ ○ ○ ○ ○
○ ○ ○ ○ ○

of team advancements

goal _____

actual _____

○ ○ ○ ○ ○
○ ○ ○ ○ ○
○ ○ ○ ○ ○
○ ○ ○ ○ ○

of customer invites

goal _____

actual _____

of business opportunity invites

goal _____

actual _____

notes

customer hot list

1.

2.

3.

4.

5.

6.

7.

8.

9.

10.

11.

12.

13.

14.

15.

16.

17.

18.

19.

20.

21.

22.

23.

24.

25.

26.

27.

28.

29.

30.

31.

32.

33.

34.

35.

36.

37.

38.

39.

40.

business hot list

1.

2.

3.

4.

5.

6.

7.

8.

9.

10.

11.

12.

13.

14.

15.

16.

17.

18.

19.

20.

21.

22.

23.

24.

25.

26.

27.

28.

29.

30.

31.

32.

33.

34.

35.

36.

37.

38.

39.

40.

week of: _____

top three yearly goals
1.
2.
3.

top three monthly goals
1.
2.
3.

top three weekly goals
1.
2.
3.

three most important
meetings/events
1.
2.
3.

	monday		tuesday	
6				
7				
8				
9				
10				
11				
12				
1				
2				
3				
4				
5				
6				
7				
8				
9				
10				
invites	business	customer	business	customer

win the week

Action	Mon	Tues	Weds	Thurs	Fri	Sat	Sun	Goal	Actual	%
Read Vision/Review Goals										
Book of Proof										

wednesday		thursday		friday		saturday		sunday		
										6
										7
										8
										9
										10
										11
										12
										1
										2
										3
										4
										5
										6
										7
										8
										9
										10
business	customer	business	customer	business	customer	business	customer	business	customer	

marketing plan

monday	tuesday	wednesday	thursday	friday	saturday	sunday

remember, life happens for you, not to you.

WINS _____

LOSSES _____

HOW CAN I IMPROVE? _____

week of: _____

top three yearly goals
1.
2.
3.

top three monthly goals
1.
2.
3.

top three weekly goals
1.
2.
3.

three most important
meetings/events
1.
2.
3.

	monday		tuesday	
6				
7				
8				
9				
10				
11				
12				
1				
2				
3				
4				
5				
6				
7				
8				
9				
10				
invites	business	customer	business	customer

win the week

Action	Mon	Tues	Weds	Thurs	Fri	Sat	Sun	Goal	Actual	%
Read Vision/Review Goals										
Book of Proof										

wednesday		thursday		friday		saturday		sunday		
										6
										7
										8
										9
										10
										11
										12
										1
										2
										3
										4
										5
										6
										7
										8
										9
										10
business	customer	business	customer	business	customer	business	customer	business	customer	

marketing plan

monday	tuesday	wednesday	thursday	friday	saturday	sunday

remember, life happens for you, not to you.

WINS _____

LOSSES _____

HOW CAN I IMPROVE? _____

week of: _____

review last week/
plan this week ☐

top three yearly goals
1.
2.
3.

top three monthly goals
1.
2.
3.

top three weekly goals
1.
2.
3.

three most important
meetings/events
1.
2.
3.

	monday		tuesday	
6				
7				
8				
9				
10				
11				
12				
1				
2				
3				
4				
5				
6				
7				
8				
9				
10				
invites	business	customer	business	customer

win the week

Action	Mon	Tues	Weds	Thurs	Fri	Sat	Sun	Goal	Actual	%
Read Vision/Review Goals										
Book of Proof										

wednesday		thursday		friday		saturday		sunday		
										6
										7
										8
										9
										10
										11
										12
										1
										2
										3
										4
										5
										6
										7
										8
										9
										10
business	customer	business	customer	business	customer	business	customer	business	customer	

marketing plan

monday	tuesday	wednesday	thursday	friday	saturday	sunday

remember, life happens for you, not to you.

WINS _____

LOSSES _____

HOW CAN I IMPROVE? _____

week of: _____

review last week/
plan this week ☐

top three yearly goals
1.
2.
3.

top three monthly goals
1.
2.
3.

top three weekly goals
1.
2.
3.

three most important
meetings/events
1.
2.
3.

6	
7	
8	
9	
10	
11	
12	
1	
2	
3	
4	
5	
6	
7	
8	
9	
10	

invites	business	customer	business	customer

win the week

Action	Mon	Tues	Weds	Thurs	Fri	Sat	Sun	Goal	Actual	%
Read Vision/Review Goals										
Book of Proof										

wednesday		thursday		friday		saturday		sunday		
										6
										7
										8
										9
										10
										11
										12
										1
										2
										3
										4
										5
										6
										7
										8
										9
										10
business	customer	business	customer	business	customer	business	customer	business	customer	

marketing plan

monday	tuesday	wednesday	thursday	friday	saturday	sunday

remember, life happens for you, not to you.

WINS _____

LOSSES _____

HOW CAN I IMPROVE? _____

week of: _____

review last week/
plan this week ☐

top three yearly goals
1.
2.
3.

top three monthly goals
1.
2.
3.

top three weekly goals
1.
2.
3.

three most important
meetings/events
1.
2.
3.

	monday		tuesday	
6				
7				
8				
9				
10				
11				
12				
1				
2				
3				
4				
5				
6				
7				
8				
9				
10				
invites	business	customer	business	customer

win the week

Action	Mon	Tues	Weds	Thurs	Fri	Sat	Sun	Goal	Actual	%
Read Vision/Review Goals										
Book of Proof										

wednesday		thursday		friday		saturday		sunday		
										6
										7
										8
										9
										10
										11
										12
										1
										2
										3
										4
										5
										6
										7
										8
										9
										10
business	customer	business	customer	business	customer	business	customer	business	customer	

marketing plan

monday	tuesday	wednesday	thursday	friday	saturday	sunday

remember, life happens for you, not to you.

WINS _____

LOSSES _____

HOW CAN I IMPROVE? _____

dream. plan. hustle. win.

monthly goals & intentions

family/home

relationships

my body

finances

business

fun/community

personal development I'm committed to

business development I'm committed to

time to reflect

biggest accomplishments
last month?

areas I need to improve
this month?

_____

_____

_____

_____

High Vibe Habit Stacker

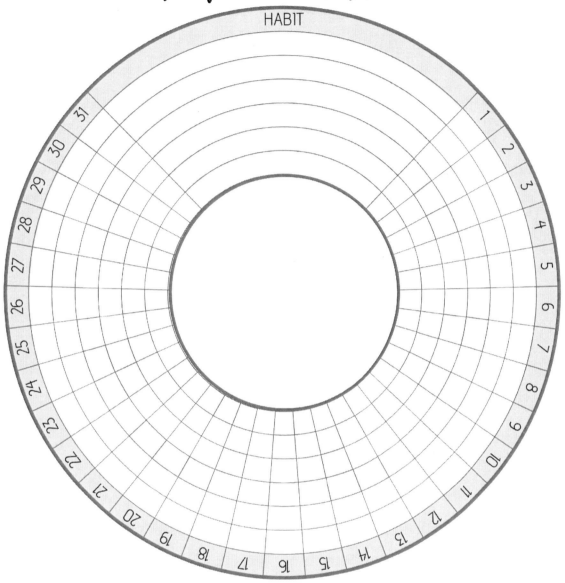

HABIT

Habit Stack	Days Complete	Percentage Complete
		%
		%
		%
		%
		%
		%

Month:

_____

Notes:

_____
_____
_____
_____
_____
_____
_____
_____
_____
_____

sunday	monday	tuesday

wednesday	thursday	friday	saturday

weekly to-do's

- [ ] _____
- [ ] _____
- [ ] _____
- [ ] _____
- [ ] _____
- [ ] _____
- [ ] _____
- [ ] _____
- [ ] _____
- [ ] _____
- [ ] _____
- [ ] _____
- [ ] _____
- [ ] _____
- [ ] _____
- [ ] _____
- [ ] _____
- [ ] _____

- [ ] _____
- [ ] _____
- [ ] _____
- [ ] _____
- [ ] _____
- [ ] _____
- [ ] _____
- [ ] _____
- [ ] _____
- [ ] _____
- [ ] _____
- [ ] _____
- [ ] _____
- [ ] _____
- [ ] _____
- [ ] _____
- [ ] _____
- [ ] _____

weekly to-do's

- [ ] _____
- [ ] _____
- [ ] _____
- [ ] _____
- [ ] _____
- [ ] _____
- [ ] _____
- [ ] _____
- [ ] _____
- [ ] _____
- [ ] _____
- [ ] _____
- [ ] _____
- [ ] _____
- [ ] _____
- [ ] _____
- [ ] _____

- [ ] _____
- [ ] _____
- [ ] _____
- [ ] _____
- [ ] _____
- [ ] _____
- [ ] _____
- [ ] _____
- [ ] _____
- [ ] _____
- [ ] _____
- [ ] _____
- [ ] _____
- [ ] _____
- [ ] _____
- [ ] _____
- [ ] _____

monthly enrollments

Date	Name						

business goals

of new customers

goal _____

actual _____

○ ○ ○ ○ ○
○ ○ ○ ○ ○
○ ○ ○ ○ ○
○ ○ ○ ○ ○

of new team members

goal _____

actual _____

○ ○ ○ ○ ○
○ ○ ○ ○ ○
○ ○ ○ ○ ○
○ ○ ○ ○ ○

of team advancements

goal _____

actual _____

○ ○ ○ ○ ○
○ ○ ○ ○ ○
○ ○ ○ ○ ○
○ ○ ○ ○ ○

of customer invites

goal _____

actual _____

of business opportunity invites

goal _____

actual _____

notes

customer hot list

1.
2.
3.
4.
5.
6.
7.
8.
9.
10.
11.
12.
13.
14.
15.
16.
17.
18.
19.
20.

21.
22.
23.
24.
25.
26.
27.
28.
29.
30.
31.
32.
33.
34.
35.
36.
37.
38.
39.
40.

business hot list

1.
2.
3.
4.
5.
6.
7.
8.
9.
10.
11.
12.
13.
14.
15.
16.
17.
18.
19.
20.

21.
22.
23.
24.
25.
26.
27.
28.
29.
30.
31.
32.
33.
34.
35.
36.
37.
38.
39.
40.

week of: _____

review last week/
plan this week ☐

top three yearly goals
1.
2.
3.

top three monthly goals
1.
2.
3.

top three weekly goals
1.
2.
3.

three most important
meetings/events
1.
2.
3.

	monday		tuesday	
6				
7				
8				
9				
10				
11				
12				
1				
2				
3				
4				
5				
6				
7				
8				
9				
10				
invites	business	customer	business	customer

win the week

Action	Mon	Tues	Weds	Thurs	Fri	Sat	Sun	Goal	Actual	%
Read Vision/Review Goals										
Book of Proof										

wednesday		thursday		friday		saturday		sunday		
										6
										7
										8
										9
										10
										11
										12
										1
										2
										3
										4
										5
										6
										7
										8
										9
										10
business	customer	business	customer	business	customer	business	customer	business	customer	

marketing plan

monday	tuesday	wednesday	thursday	friday	saturday	sunday

remember, life happens for you, not to you.

WINS _____

LOSSES _____

HOW CAN I IMPROVE? _____

week of: _____

top three yearly goals
1.
2.
3.

top three monthly goals
1.
2.
3.

top three weekly goals
1.
2.
3.

three most important
meetings/events
1.
2.
3.

	monday		tuesday	
6				
7				
8				
9				
10				
11				
12				
1				
2				
3				
4				
5				
6				
7				
8				
9				
10				
invites	business	customer	business	customer

win the week

Action	Mon	Tues	Weds	Thurs	Fri	Sat	Sun	Goal	Actual	%
Read Vision/Review Goals										
Book of Proof										

wednesday		thursday		friday		saturday		sunday		
										6
										7
										8
										9
										10
										11
										12
										1
										2
										3
										4
										5
										6
										7
										8
										9
										10
business	customer	business	customer	business	customer	business	customer	business	customer	

marketing plan

monday	tuesday	wednesday	thursday	friday	saturday	sunday

remember, life happens for you, not to you.

WINS _____

LOSSES _____

HOW CAN I IMPROVE? _____

week of: _____

| review last week/ plan this week | ☐ |

top three yearly goals
1.
2.
3.

top three monthly goals
1.
2.
3.

top three weekly goals
1.
2.
3.

three most important
meetings/events
1.
2.
3.

	monday		tuesday	
6				
7				
8				
9				
10				
11				
12				
1				
2				
3				
4				
5				
6				
7				
8				
9				
10				
invites	business	customer	business	customer

win the week

Action	Mon	Tues	Weds	Thurs	Fri	Sat	Sun	Goal	Actual	%
Read Vision/Review Goals										
Book of Proof										

wednesday		thursday		friday		saturday		sunday		
										6
										7
										8
										9
										10
										11
										12
										1
										2
										3
										4
										5
										6
										7
										8
										9
										10
business	customer	business	customer	business	customer	business	customer	business	customer	

marketing plan

monday	tuesday	wednesday	thursday	friday	saturday	sunday

remember, life happens for you, not to you.

WINS _____

LOSSES _____

HOW CAN I IMPROVE? _____

week of: _____

top three yearly goals
1.
2.
3.

top three monthly goals
1.
2.
3.

top three weekly goals
1.
2.
3.

three most important
meetings/events
1.
2.
3.

	monday ☐		tuesday ☐	
6				
7				
8				
9				
10				
11				
12				
1				
2				
3				
4				
5				
6				
7				
8				
9				
10				
invites	business	customer	business	customer

win the week

Action	Mon	Tues	Weds	Thurs	Fri	Sat	Sun	Goal	Actual	%
Read Vision/Review Goals										
Book of Proof										

wednesday		thursday		friday		saturday		sunday		
										6
										7
										8
										9
										10
										11
										12
										1
										2
										3
										4
										5
										6
										7
										8
										9
										10
business	customer	business	customer	business	customer	business	customer	business	customer	

marketing plan

monday	tuesday	wednesday	thursday	friday	saturday	sunday

remember, life happens for you, not to you.

WINS _____

LOSSES _____

HOW CAN I IMPROVE? _____

week of: _____

| review last week/ plan this week | ☐ |

top three yearly goals
1.
2.
3.

top three monthly goals
1.
2.
3.

top three weekly goals
1.
2.
3.

three most important
meetings/events
1.
2.
3.

	monday		tuesday	
6				
7				
8				
9				
10				
11				
12				
1				
2				
3				
4				
5				
6				
7				
8				
9				
10				
invites	business	customer	business	customer

win the week

Action	Mon	Tues	Weds	Thurs	Fri	Sat	Sun	Goal	Actual	%
Read Vision/Review Goals										
Book of Proof										

wednesday		thursday		friday		saturday		sunday		
										6
										7
										8
										9
										10
										11
										12
										1
										2
										3
										4
										5
										6
										7
										8
										9
										10
business	customer	business	customer	business	customer	business	customer	business	customer	

marketing plan

monday	tuesday	wednesday	thursday	friday	saturday	sunday

remember, life happens for you, not to you.

WINS _____

LOSSES _____

HOW CAN I IMPROVE? _____

Month:

dream. plan. hustle. win.

monthly goals & intentions

family/home

relationships

my body

finances

business

fun/community

personal development I'm committed to

business development I'm committed to

time to reflect

biggest accomplishments
last month?

areas I need to improve
this month?

_____

_____

_____

_____

High Vibe Habit Stacker

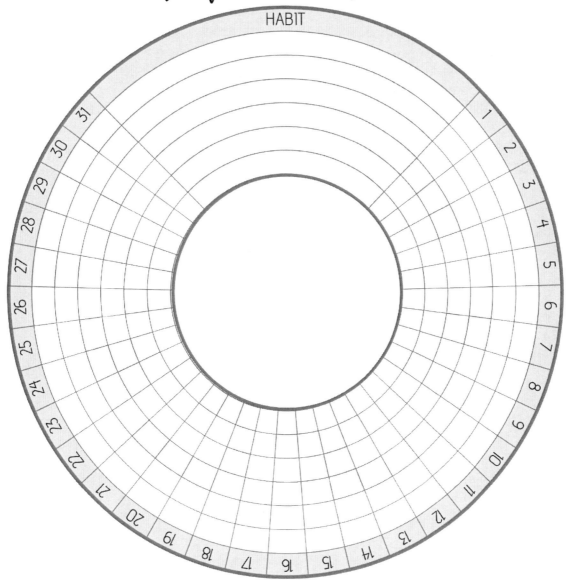

HABIT

Habit Stack	Days Complete	Percentage Complete
		%
		%
		%
		%
		%
		%

Month:

_____

Notes:

_____

_____

_____

_____

_____

_____

_____

_____

_____

_____

sunday	monday	tuesday

wednesday	thursday	friday	saturday

weekly to-do's

- [ ] _____
- [ ] _____
- [ ] _____
- [ ] _____
- [ ] _____
- [ ] _____
- [ ] _____
- [ ] _____
- [ ] _____
- [ ] _____
- [ ] _____
- [ ] _____
- [ ] _____
- [ ] _____
- [ ] _____
- [ ] _____
- [ ] _____
- [ ] _____

- [ ] _____
- [ ] _____
- [ ] _____
- [ ] _____
- [ ] _____
- [ ] _____
- [ ] _____
- [ ] _____
- [ ] _____
- [ ] _____
- [ ] _____
- [ ] _____
- [ ] _____
- [ ] _____
- [ ] _____
- [ ] _____
- [ ] _____
- [ ] _____

weekly to-do's

- [ ] _____
- [ ] _____
- [ ] _____
- [ ] _____
- [ ] _____
- [ ] _____
- [ ] _____
- [ ] _____
- [ ] _____
- [ ] _____
- [ ] _____
- [ ] _____
- [ ] _____
- [ ] _____
- [ ] _____
- [ ] _____
- [ ] _____

- [ ] _____
- [ ] _____
- [ ] _____
- [ ] _____
- [ ] _____
- [ ] _____
- [ ] _____
- [ ] _____
- [ ] _____
- [ ] _____
- [ ] _____
- [ ] _____
- [ ] _____
- [ ] _____
- [ ] _____
- [ ] _____
- [ ] _____

monthly enrollments

Date	Name						

business goals

of new customers

goal _____

actual _____

○ ○ ○ ○ ○
○ ○ ○ ○ ○
○ ○ ○ ○ ○
○ ○ ○ ○ ○

of new team members

goal _____

actual _____

○ ○ ○ ○ ○
○ ○ ○ ○ ○
○ ○ ○ ○ ○
○ ○ ○ ○ ○

of team advancements

goal _____

actual _____

○ ○ ○ ○ ○
○ ○ ○ ○ ○
○ ○ ○ ○ ○
○ ○ ○ ○ ○

of customer invites

goal _____

actual _____

of business opportunity invites

goal _____

actual _____

notes

customer hot list

1.	21.
2.	22.
3.	23.
4.	24.
5.	25.
6.	26.
7.	27.
8.	28.
9.	29.
10.	30.
11.	31.
12.	32.
13.	33.
14.	34.
15.	35.
16.	36.
17.	37.
18.	38.
19.	39.
20.	40.

business hot list

1.

2.

3.

4.

5.

6.

7.

8.

9.

10.

11.

12.

13.

14.

15.

16.

17.

18.

19.

20.

21.

22.

23.

24.

25.

26.

27.

28.

29.

30.

31.

32.

33.

34.

35.

36.

37.

38.

39.

40.

week of: _____

| review last week/ plan this week | ☐ |

top three yearly goals
1.
2.
3.

top three monthly goals
1.
2.
3.

top three weekly goals
1.
2.
3.

three most important
meetings/events
1.
2.
3.

	monday ☐		tuesday ☐	
6				
7				
8				
9				
10				
11				
12				
1				
2				
3				
4				
5				
6				
7				
8				
9				
10				
invites	business	customer	business	customer

win the week

Action	Mon	Tues	Weds	Thurs	Fri	Sat	Sun	Goal	Actual	%
Read Vision/Review Goals										
Book of Proof										

wednesday		thursday		friday		saturday		sunday		
										6
										7
										8
										9
										10
										11
										12
										1
										2
										3
										4
										5
										6
										7
										8
										9
										10
business	customer	business	customer	business	customer	business	customer	business	customer	

marketing plan

monday	tuesday	wednesday	thursday	friday	saturday	sunday

remember, life happens for you, not to you.

WINS _____

LOSSES _____

HOW CAN I IMPROVE? _____

week of: _____

top three yearly goals
1.
2.
3.

top three monthly goals
1.
2.
3.

top three weekly goals
1.
2.
3.

three most important
meetings/events
1.
2.
3.

	monday		tuesday	
6				
7				
8				
9				
10				
11				
12				
1				
2				
3				
4				
5				
6				
7				
8				
9				
10				
invites	business	customer	business	customer

win the week

Action	Mon	Tues	Weds	Thurs	Fri	Sat	Sun	Goal	Actual	%
Read Vision/Review Goals										
Book of Proof										

wednesday	thursday	friday	saturday	sunday	
					6
					7
					8
					9
					10
					11
					12
					1
					2
					3
					4
					5
					6
					7
					8
					9
					10

business	customer	business	customer	business	customer	business	customer	business	customer

marketing plan

monday	tuesday	wednesday	thursday	friday	saturday	sunday

remember, life happens for you, not to you.

WINS _____

LOSSES _____

HOW CAN I IMPROVE? _____

week of: _____

top three yearly goals
1.
2.
3.

top three monthly goals
1.
2.
3.

top three weekly goals
1.
2.
3.

three most important
meetings/events
1.
2.
3.

	monday		tuesday	
6				
7				
8				
9				
10				
11				
12				
1				
2				
3				
4				
5				
6				
7				
8				
9				
10				
invites	business	customer	business	customer

win the week

Action	Mon	Tues	Weds	Thurs	Fri	Sat	Sun	Goal	Actual	%
Read Vision/Review Goals										
Book of Proof										

wednesday		thursday		friday		saturday		sunday		
										6
										7
										8
										9
										10
										11
										12
										1
										2
										3
										4
										5
										6
										7
										8
										9
										10
business	customer	business	customer	business	customer	business	customer	business	customer	

marketing plan

monday	tuesday	wednesday	thursday	friday	saturday	sunday

remember, life happens for you, not to you.

WINS _____

LOSSES _____

HOW CAN I IMPROVE? _____

week of: _____

review last week/
plan this week ☐

top three yearly goals
1.
2.
3.

top three monthly goals
1.
2.
3.

top three weekly goals
1.
2.
3.

three most important
meetings/events
1.
2.
3.

	monday		tuesday	
6				
7				
8				
9				
10				
11				
12				
1				
2				
3				
4				
5				
6				
7				
8				
9				
10				
invites	business	customer	business	customer

win the week

Action	Mon	Tues	Weds	Thurs	Fri	Sat	Sun	Goal	Actual	%
Read Vision/Review Goals										
Book of Proof										

wednesday		thursday		friday		saturday		sunday		
										6
										7
										8
										9
										10
										11
										12
										1
										2
										3
										4
										5
										6
										7
										8
										9
										10
business	customer	business	customer	business	customer	business	customer	business	customer	

marketing plan

monday	tuesday	wednesday	thursday	friday	saturday	sunday

remember, life happens for you, not to you.

WINS _____

LOSSES _____

HOW CAN I IMPROVE? _____

week of: _____

review last week/ plan this week ☐

top three yearly goals
1.
2.
3.

top three monthly goals
1.
2.
3.

top three weekly goals
1.
2.
3.

three most important
meetings/events
1.
2.
3.

	monday		tuesday	
6				
7				
8				
9				
10				
11				
12				
1				
2				
3				
4				
5				
6				
7				
8				
9				
10				
invites	business	customer	business	customer

win the week

Action	Mon	Tues	Weds	Thurs	Fri	Sat	Sun	Goal	Actual	%
Read Vision/Review Goals										
Book of Proof										

wednesday	thursday	friday	saturday	sunday	
					6
					7
					8
					9
					10
					11
					12
					1
					2
					3
					4
					5
					6
					7
					8
					9
					10

business	customer	business	customer	business	customer	business	customer	business	customer

marketing plan

monday	tuesday	wednesday	thursday	friday	saturday	sunday

remember, life happens for you, not to you.

WINS _____

LOSSES _____

HOW CAN I IMPROVE? _____

Month:

dream. plan. hustle. win.

monthly goals & intentions

family/home

relationships

my body

finances

business

fun/community

personal development I'm committed to

business development I'm committed to

time to reflect

biggest accomplishments
last month?

areas I need to improve
this month?

_____

_____

_____

_____

High Vibe Habit Stacker

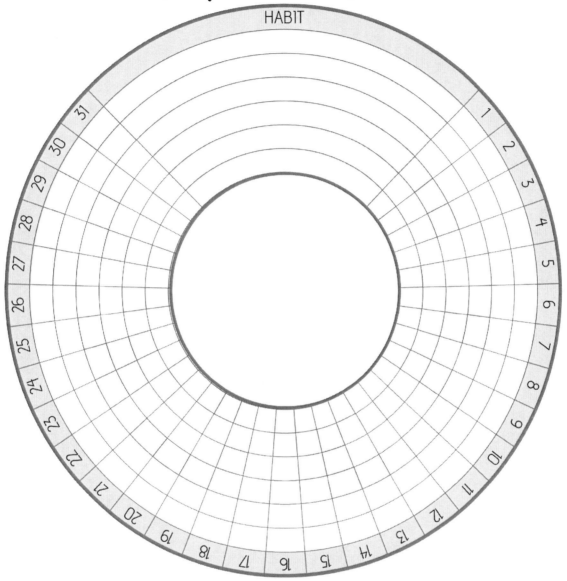

HABIT

Habit Stack	Days Complete	Percentage Complete
		%
		%
		%
		%
		%
		%

Month:

_____

Notes:

_____

_____

_____

_____

_____

_____

_____

_____

_____

_____

sunday	monday	tuesday

wednesday	thursday	friday	saturday

weekly to-do's

☐ _____

☐ _____

☐ _____

☐ _____

☐ _____

☐ _____

☐ _____

☐ _____

☐ _____

☐ _____

☐ _____

☐ _____

☐ _____

☐ _____

☐ _____

☐ _____

☐ _____

☐ _____

☐ _____

☐ _____

☐ _____

☐ _____

☐ _____

☐ _____

☐ _____

☐ _____

☐ _____

☐ _____

☐ _____

☐ _____

☐ _____

☐ _____

☐ _____

☐ _____

☐ _____

weekly to-do's

- [ ] _____
- [ ] _____
- [ ] _____
- [ ] _____
- [ ] _____
- [ ] _____
- [ ] _____
- [ ] _____
- [ ] _____
- [ ] _____
- [ ] _____
- [ ] _____
- [ ] _____
- [ ] _____
- [ ] _____
- [ ] _____
- [ ] _____

- [ ] _____
- [ ] _____
- [ ] _____
- [ ] _____
- [ ] _____
- [ ] _____
- [ ] _____
- [ ] _____
- [ ] _____
- [ ] _____
- [ ] _____
- [ ] _____
- [ ] _____
- [ ] _____
- [ ] _____
- [ ] _____
- [ ] _____

monthly enrollments

Date	Name						

business goals

of new customers

goal _____

actual _____

○ ○ ○ ○ ○
○ ○ ○ ○ ○
○ ○ ○ ○ ○
○ ○ ○ ○ ○

of new team members

goal _____

actual _____

○ ○ ○ ○ ○
○ ○ ○ ○ ○
○ ○ ○ ○ ○
○ ○ ○ ○ ○

of team advancements

goal _____

actual _____

○ ○ ○ ○ ○
○ ○ ○ ○ ○
○ ○ ○ ○ ○
○ ○ ○ ○ ○

of customer invites

goal _____

actual _____

of business opportunity invites

goal _____

actual _____

notes

customer hot list

1.
2.
3.
4.
5.
6.
7.
8.
9.
10.
11.
12.
13.
14.
15.
16.
17.
18.
19.
20.

21.
22.
23.
24.
25.
26.
27.
28.
29.
30.
31.
32.
33.
34.
35.
36.
37.
38.
39.
40.

business hot list

1.	21.
2.	22.
3.	23.
4.	24.
5.	25.
6.	26.
7.	27.
8.	28.
9.	29.
10.	30.
11.	31.
12.	32.
13.	33.
14.	34.
15.	35.
16.	36.
17.	37.
18.	38.
19.	39.
20.	40.

week of: _____

top three yearly goals
1.
2.
3.

top three monthly goals
1.
2.
3.

top three weekly goals
1.
2.
3.

three most important
meetings/events
1.
2.
3.

	monday		tuesday	
6				
7				
8				
9				
10				
11				
12				
1				
2				
3				
4				
5				
6				
7				
8				
9				
10				
invites	business	customer	business	customer

win the week

Action	Mon	Tues	Weds	Thurs	Fri	Sat	Sun	Goal	Actual	%
Read Vision/Review Goals										
Book of Proof										

wednesday		thursday		friday		saturday		sunday		
										6
										7
										8
										9
										10
										11
										12
										1
										2
										3
										4
										5
										6
										7
										8
										9
										10
business	customer	business	customer	business	customer	business	customer	business	customer	

marketing plan

monday	tuesday	wednesday	thursday	friday	saturday	sunday

remember, life happens for you, not to you.

WINS _____

LOSSES _____

HOW CAN I IMPROVE? _____

week of: _____

top three yearly goals
1.
2.
3.

top three monthly goals
1.
2.
3.

top three weekly goals
1.
2.
3.

three most important
meetings/events
1.
2.
3.

	monday		tuesday	
6				
7				
8				
9				
10				
11				
12				
1				
2				
3				
4				
5				
6				
7				
8				
9				
10				
invites	business	customer	business	customer

win the week

Action	Mon	Tues	Weds	Thurs	Fri	Sat	Sun	Goal	Actual	%
Read Vision/Review Goals										
Book of Proof										

wednesday		thursday		friday		saturday		sunday		
										6
										7
										8
										9
										10
										11
										12
										1
										2
										3
										4
										5
										6
										7
										8
										9
										10
business	customer	business	customer	business	customer	business	customer	business	customer	

marketing plan

monday	tuesday	wednesday	thursday	friday	saturday	sunday

remember, life happens for you, not to you.

WINS _____

LOSSES _____

HOW CAN I IMPROVE? _____

week of: _____

top three yearly goals
1.
2.
3.

top three monthly goals
1.
2.
3.

top three weekly goals
1.
2.
3.

three most important
meetings/events
1.
2.
3.

	monday ☐		tuesday ☐	
6				
7				
8				
9				
10				
11				
12				
1				
2				
3				
4				
5				
6				
7				
8				
9				
10				
invites	business	customer	business	customer

win the week

Action	Mon	Tues	Weds	Thurs	Fri	Sat	Sun	Goal	Actual	%
Read Vision/Review Goals										
Book of Proof										

wednesday		thursday		friday		saturday		sunday		
										6
										7
										8
										9
										10
										11
										12
										1
										2
										3
										4
										5
										6
										7
										8
										9
										10
business	customer	business	customer	business	customer	business	customer	business	customer	

marketing plan

monday	tuesday	wednesday	thursday	friday	saturday	sunday

remember, life happens for you, not to you.

WINS _____

LOSSES _____

HOW CAN I IMPROVE? _____

week of: _____

top three yearly goals
1.
2.
3.

top three monthly goals
1.
2.
3.

top three weekly goals
1.
2.
3.

three most important
meetings/events
1.
2.
3.

	monday		tuesday	
6				
7				
8				
9				
10				
11				
12				
1				
2				
3				
4				
5				
6				
7				
8				
9				
10				
invites	business	customer	business	customer

win the week

Action	Mon	Tues	Weds	Thurs	Fri	Sat	Sun	Goal	Actual	%
Read Vision/Review Goals										
Book of Proof										

wednesday		thursday		friday		saturday		sunday		
										6
										7
										8
										9
										10
										11
										12
										1
										2
										3
										4
										5
										6
										7
										8
										9
										10
business	customer	business	customer	business	customer	business	customer	business	customer	

marketing plan

monday	tuesday	wednesday	thursday	friday	saturday	sunday

remember, life happens for you, not to you.

WINS _____

LOSSES _____

HOW CAN I IMPROVE? _____

week of: _____

top three yearly goals
1.
2.
3.

top three monthly goals
1.
2.
3.

top three weekly goals
1.
2.
3.

three most important
meetings/events
1.
2.
3.

	monday		tuesday	
6				
7				
8				
9				
10				
11				
12				
1				
2				
3				
4				
5				
6				
7				
8				
9				
10				
invites	business	customer	business	customer

win the week

Action	Mon	Tues	Weds	Thurs	Fri	Sat	Sun	Goal	Actual	%
Read Vision/Review Goals										
Book of Proof										

wednesday		thursday		friday		saturday		sunday		
										6
										7
										8
										9
										10
										11
										12
										1
										2
										3
										4
										5
										6
										7
										8
										9
										10
business	customer	business	customer	business	customer	business	customer	business	customer	

marketing plan

monday	tuesday	wednesday	thursday	friday	saturday	sunday

remember, life happens for you, not to you.

WINS _____

LOSSES _____

HOW CAN I IMPROVE? _____

Month:

dream. plan. hustle. win.

monthly goals & intentions

family/home

relationships

my body

finances

business

fun/community

personal development I'm committed to

business development I'm committed to

time to reflect

biggest accomplishments
last month?

areas I need to improve
this month?

_____

_____

_____

_____

High Vibe Habit Stacker

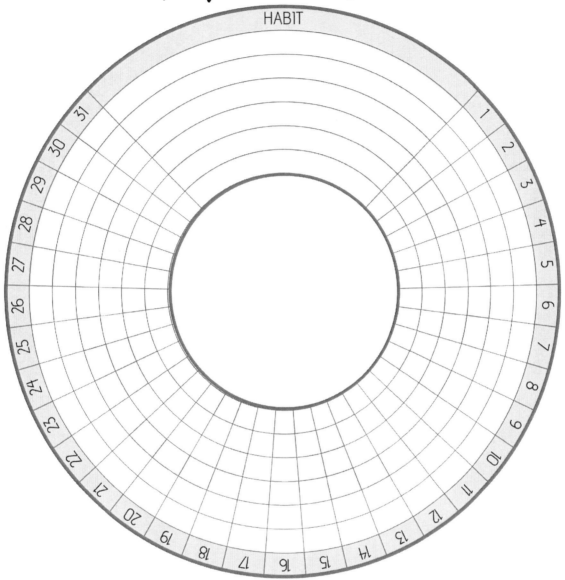

HABIT

Habit Stack	Days Complete	Percentage Complete
		%
		%
		%
		%
		%
		%

Month:

_____

Notes:

_____

_____

_____

_____

_____

_____

_____

_____

_____

_____

sunday	monday	tuesday

wednesday	thursday	friday	saturday

weekly to-do's

☐ _____
☐ _____
☐ _____
☐ _____
☐ _____
☐ _____
☐ _____
☐ _____
☐ _____
☐ _____
☐ _____
☐ _____
☐ _____
☐ _____
☐ _____
☐ _____
☐ _____

☐ _____
☐ _____
☐ _____
☐ _____
☐ _____
☐ _____
☐ _____
☐ _____
☐ _____
☐ _____
☐ _____
☐ _____
☐ _____
☐ _____
☐ _____
☐ _____
☐ _____

weekly to-do's

- [ ] _____
- [ ] _____
- [ ] _____
- [ ] _____
- [ ] _____
- [ ] _____
- [ ] _____
- [ ] _____
- [ ] _____
- [ ] _____
- [ ] _____
- [ ] _____
- [ ] _____
- [ ] _____
- [ ] _____
- [ ] _____
- [ ] _____

- [ ] _____
- [ ] _____
- [ ] _____
- [ ] _____
- [ ] _____
- [ ] _____
- [ ] _____
- [ ] _____
- [ ] _____
- [ ] _____
- [ ] _____
- [ ] _____
- [ ] _____
- [ ] _____
- [ ] _____
- [ ] _____
- [ ] _____

monthly enrollments

Date	Name						

business goals

of new customers

goal _____

actual _____

○ ○ ○ ○ ○
○ ○ ○ ○ ○
○ ○ ○ ○ ○
○ ○ ○ ○ ○

of new team members

goal _____

actual _____

○ ○ ○ ○ ○
○ ○ ○ ○ ○
○ ○ ○ ○ ○
○ ○ ○ ○ ○

of team advancements

goal _____

actual _____

○ ○ ○ ○ ○
○ ○ ○ ○ ○
○ ○ ○ ○ ○
○ ○ ○ ○ ○

of customer invites

goal _____

actual _____

of business opportunity invites

goal _____

actual _____

notes

customer hot list

1.	21.
2.	22.
3.	23.
4.	24.
5.	25.
6.	26.
7.	27.
8.	28.
9.	29.
10.	30.
11.	31.
12.	32.
13.	33.
14.	34.
15.	35.
16.	36.
17.	37.
18.	38.
19.	39.
20.	40.

business hot list

1.

2.

3.

4.

5.

6.

7.

8.

9.

10.

11.

12.

13.

14.

15.

16.

17.

18.

19.

20.

21.

22.

23.

24.

25.

26.

27.

28.

29.

30.

31.

32.

33.

34.

35.

36.

37.

38.

39.

40.

week of: _____

review last week/
plan this week ☐

top three yearly goals
1.
2.
3.

top three monthly goals
1.
2.
3.

top three weekly goals
1.
2.
3.

three most important
meetings/events
1.
2.
3.

	monday		tuesday	
6				
7				
8				
9				
10				
11				
12				
1				
2				
3				
4				
5				
6				
7				
8				
9				
10				
invites	business	customer	business	customer

win the week

Action	Mon	Tues	Weds	Thurs	Fri	Sat	Sun	Goal	Actual	%
Read Vision/Review Goals										
Book of Proof										

wednesday		thursday		friday		saturday		sunday		
										6
										7
										8
										9
										10
										11
										12
										1
										2
										3
										4
										5
										6
										7
										8
										9
										10
business	customer	business	customer	business	customer	business	customer	business	customer	

marketing plan

monday	tuesday	wednesday	thursday	friday	saturday	sunday

remember, life happens for you, not to you.

WINS _____

LOSSES _____

HOW CAN I IMPROVE? _____

week of: _____

top three yearly goals
1.
2.
3.

top three monthly goals
1.
2.
3.

top three weekly goals
1.
2.
3.

three most important
meetings/events
1.
2.
3.

	monday		tuesday	
6				
7				
8				
9				
10				
11				
12				
1				
2				
3				
4				
5				
6				
7				
8				
9				
10				
invites	business	customer	business	customer

win the week

Action	Mon	Tues	Weds	Thurs	Fri	Sat	Sun	Goal	Actual	%
Read Vision/Review Goals										
Book of Proof										

wednesday		thursday		friday		saturday		sunday		
										6
										7
										8
										9
										10
										11
										12
										1
										2
										3
										4
										5
										6
										7
										8
										9
										10
business	customer	business	customer	business	customer	business	customer	business	customer	

marketing plan

monday	tuesday	wednesday	thursday	friday	saturday	sunday

remember, life happens for you, not to you.

WINS _____

LOSSES _____

HOW CAN I IMPROVE? _____

week of: _____

review last week/
plan this week ☐

top three yearly goals
1.
2.
3.

top three monthly goals
1.
2.
3.

top three weekly goals
1.
2.
3.

three most important
meetings/events
1.
2.
3.

	monday		tuesday	
6				
7				
8				
9				
10				
11				
12				
1				
2				
3				
4				
5				
6				
7				
8				
9				
10				
invites	business	customer	business	customer

win the week

Action	Mon	Tues	Weds	Thurs	Fri	Sat	Sun	Goal	Actual	%
Read Vision/Review Goals										
Book of Proof										

wednesday		thursday		friday		saturday		sunday		
										6
										7
										8
										9
										10
										11
										12
										1
										2
										3
										4
										5
										6
										7
										8
										9
										10
business	customer	business	customer	business	customer	business	customer	business	customer	

marketing plan

monday	tuesday	wednesday	thursday	friday	saturday	sunday

remember, life happens for you, not to you.

WINS _____

LOSSES _____

HOW CAN I IMPROVE? _____

week of: _____

review last week/ plan this week	☐

top three yearly goals
1.
2.
3.

top three monthly goals
1.
2.
3.

top three weekly goals
1.
2.
3.

three most important
meetings/events
1.
2.
3.

	monday		tuesday	
6				
7				
8				
9				
10				
11				
12				
1				
2				
3				
4				
5				
6				
7				
8				
9				
10				
invites	business	customer	business	customer

win the week

Action	Mon	Tues	Weds	Thurs	Fri	Sat	Sun	Goal	Actual	%
Read Vision/Review Goals										
Book of Proof										

wednesday		thursday		friday		saturday		sunday		
										6
										7
										8
										9
										10
										11
										12
										1
										2
										3
										4
										5
										6
										7
										8
										9
										10
business	customer	business	customer	business	customer	business	customer	business	customer	

marketing plan

monday	tuesday	wednesday	thursday	friday	saturday	sunday

remember, life happens for you, not to you.

WINS _____

LOSSES _____

HOW CAN I IMPROVE? _____

week of: _____

review last week/ plan this week ☐

top three yearly goals
1.
2.
3.

top three monthly goals
1.
2.
3.

top three weekly goals
1.
2.
3.

three most important
meetings/events
1.
2.
3.

	monday		tuesday	
6				
7				
8				
9				
10				
11				
12				
1				
2				
3				
4				
5				
6				
7				
8				
9				
10				
invites	business	customer	business	customer

win the week

Action	Mon	Tues	Weds	Thurs	Fri	Sat	Sun	Goal	Actual	%
Read Vision/Review Goals										
Book of Proof										

wednesday		thursday		friday		saturday		sunday		
										6
										7
										8
										9
										10
										11
										12
										1
										2
										3
										4
										5
										6
										7
										8
										9
										10
business	customer	business	customer	business	customer	business	customer	business	customer	

marketing plan

monday	tuesday	wednesday	thursday	friday	saturday	sunday

remember, life happens for you, not to you.

WINS _____

LOSSES _____

HOW CAN I IMPROVE? _____

Month:

dream. plan. hustle. win.

monthly goals & intentions

family/home

relationships

my body

finances

business

fun/community

personal development I'm committed to

business development I'm committed to

time to reflect

biggest accomplishments
last month?

areas I need to improve
this month?

_____

_____

_____

_____

High Vibe Habit Stacker

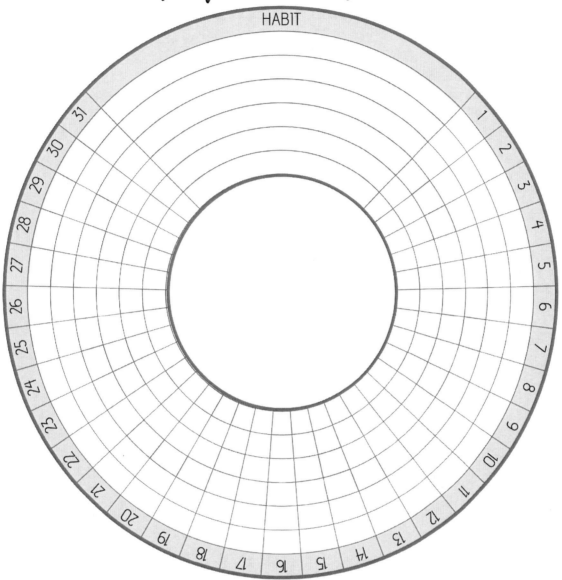

HABIT

Habit Stack	Days Complete	Percentage Complete
		%
		%
		%
		%
		%
		%

Month:

_____

Notes:

_____

_____

_____

_____

_____

_____

_____

_____

_____

_____

sunday	monday	tuesday

wednesday	thursday	friday	saturday

weekly to-do's

- [ ] _____
- [ ] _____
- [ ] _____
- [ ] _____
- [ ] _____
- [ ] _____
- [ ] _____
- [ ] _____
- [ ] _____
- [ ] _____
- [ ] _____
- [ ] _____
- [ ] _____
- [ ] _____
- [ ] _____
- [ ] _____
- [ ] _____

- [ ] _____
- [ ] _____
- [ ] _____
- [ ] _____
- [ ] _____
- [ ] _____
- [ ] _____
- [ ] _____
- [ ] _____
- [ ] _____
- [ ] _____
- [ ] _____
- [ ] _____
- [ ] _____
- [ ] _____
- [ ] _____
- [ ] _____

weekly to-do's

- [ ] _____
- [ ] _____
- [ ] _____
- [ ] _____
- [ ] _____
- [ ] _____
- [ ] _____
- [ ] _____
- [ ] _____
- [ ] _____
- [ ] _____
- [ ] _____
- [ ] _____
- [ ] _____
- [ ] _____
- [ ] _____
- [ ] _____

- [ ] _____
- [ ] _____
- [ ] _____
- [ ] _____
- [ ] _____
- [ ] _____
- [ ] _____
- [ ] _____
- [ ] _____
- [ ] _____
- [ ] _____
- [ ] _____
- [ ] _____
- [ ] _____
- [ ] _____
- [ ] _____
- [ ] _____

monthly enrollments

Date	Name						

business goals

of new customers

goal _____

actual _____

○ ○ ○ ○ ○
○ ○ ○ ○ ○
○ ○ ○ ○ ○
○ ○ ○ ○ ○

of new team members

goal _____

actual _____

○ ○ ○ ○ ○
○ ○ ○ ○ ○
○ ○ ○ ○ ○
○ ○ ○ ○ ○

of team advancements

goal _____

actual _____

○ ○ ○ ○ ○
○ ○ ○ ○ ○
○ ○ ○ ○ ○
○ ○ ○ ○ ○

of customer invites

goal _____

actual _____

of business opportunity invites

goal _____

actual _____

notes

customer hot list

1.
2.
3.
4.
5.
6.
7.
8.
9.
10.
11.
12.
13.
14.
15.
16.
17.
18.
19.
20.

21.
22.
23.
24.
25.
26.
27.
28.
29.
30.
31.
32.
33.
34.
35.
36.
37.
38.
39.
40.

business hot list

1.

2.

3.

4.

5.

6.

7.

8.

9.

10.

11.

12.

13.

14.

15.

16.

17.

18.

19.

20.

21.

22.

23.

24.

25.

26.

27.

28.

29.

30.

31.

32.

33.

34.

35.

36.

37.

38.

39.

40.

week of: _____

review last week/
plan this week ☐

top three yearly goals
1.
2.
3.

top three monthly goals
1.
2.
3.

top three weekly goals
1.
2.
3.

three most important
meetings/events
1.
2.
3.

	monday		tuesday	
6				
7				
8				
9				
10				
11				
12				
1				
2				
3				
4				
5				
6				
7				
8				
9				
10				
invites	business	customer	business	customer

win the week

Action	Mon	Tues	Weds	Thurs	Fri	Sat	Sun	Goal	Actual	%
Read Vision/Review Goals										
Book of Proof										

wednesday		thursday		friday		saturday		sunday		
										6
										7
										8
										9
										10
										11
										12
										1
										2
										3
										4
										5
										6
										7
										8
										9
										10
business	customer	business	customer	business	customer	business	customer	business	customer	

marketing plan

monday	tuesday	wednesday	thursday	friday	saturday	sunday

remember, life happens for you, not to you.

WINS _____

LOSSES _____

HOW CAN I IMPROVE? _____

week of: _____

top three yearly goals
1.
2.
3.

top three monthly goals
1.
2.
3.

top three weekly goals
1.
2.
3.

three most important
meetings/events
1.
2.
3.

	monday ☐		tuesday ☐	
6				
7				
8				
9				
10				
11				
12				
1				
2				
3				
4				
5				
6				
7				
8				
9				
10				
invites	business	customer	business	customer

win the week

Action	Mon	Tues	Weds	Thurs	Fri	Sat	Sun	Goal	Actual	%
Read Vision/Review Goals										
Book of Proof										

wednesday		thursday		friday		saturday		sunday		
										6
										7
										8
										9
										10
										11
										12
										1
										2
										3
										4
										5
										6
										7
										8
										9
										10
business	customer	business	customer	business	customer	business	customer	business	customer	

marketing plan

monday	tuesday	wednesday	thursday	friday	saturday	sunday

remember, life happens for you, not to you.

WINS _____

LOSSES _____

HOW CAN I IMPROVE? _____

week of: _____

top three yearly goals
1.
2.
3.

top three monthly goals
1.
2.
3.

top three weekly goals
1.
2.
3.

three most important
meetings/events
1.
2.
3.

	monday ☐		tuesday ☐	
6				
7				
8				
9				
10				
11				
12				
1				
2				
3				
4				
5				
6				
7				
8				
9				
10				
invites	business	customer	business	customer

win the week

Action	Mon	Tues	Weds	Thurs	Fri	Sat	Sun	Goal	Actual	%
Read Vision/Review Goals										
Book of Proof										

wednesday		thursday		friday		saturday		sunday		
										6
										7
										8
										9
										10
										11
										12
										1
										2
										3
										4
										5
										6
										7
										8
										9
										10
business	customer	business	customer	business	customer	business	customer	business	customer	

marketing plan

monday	tuesday	wednesday	thursday	friday	saturday	sunday

remember, life happens for you, not to you.

WINS _____

LOSSES _____

HOW CAN I IMPROVE? _____

week of: _____

review last week/
plan this week ☐

top three yearly goals
1.
2.
3.

top three monthly goals
1.
2.
3.

top three weekly goals
1.
2.
3.

three most important
meetings/events
1.
2.
3.

	monday		tuesday	
6				
7				
8				
9				
10				
11				
12				
1				
2				
3				
4				
5				
6				
7				
8				
9				
10				
invites	business	customer	business	customer

win the week

Action	Mon	Tues	Weds	Thurs	Fri	Sat	Sun	Goal	Actual	%
Read Vision/Review Goals										
Book of Proof										

wednesday		thursday		friday		saturday		sunday		
										6
										7
										8
										9
										10
										11
										12
										1
										2
										3
										4
										5
										6
										7
										8
										9
										10
business	customer	business	customer	business	customer	business	customer	business	customer	

marketing plan

monday	tuesday	wednesday	thursday	friday	saturday	sunday

remember, life happens for you, not to you.

WINS _____

LOSSES _____

HOW CAN I IMPROVE? _____

week of: _____

review last week/ plan this week	☐

top three yearly goals
1.
2.
3.

top three monthly goals
1.
2.
3.

top three weekly goals
1.
2.
3.

three most important meetings/events
1.
2.
3.

	monday		tuesday	
6				
7				
8				
9				
10				
11				
12				
1				
2				
3				
4				
5				
6				
7				
8				
9				
10				
invites	business	customer	business	customer

win the week

Action	Mon	Tues	Weds	Thurs	Fri	Sat	Sun	Goal	Actual	%
Read Vision/Review Goals										
Book of Proof										

wednesday		thursday		friday		saturday		sunday		
										6
										7
										8
										9
										10
										11
										12
										1
										2
										3
										4
										5
										6
										7
										8
										9
										10
business	customer	business	customer	business	customer	business	customer	business	customer	

marketing plan

monday	tuesday	wednesday	thursday	friday	saturday	sunday

remember, life happens for you, not to you.

WINS _____

LOSSES _____

HOW CAN I IMPROVE? _____

Month:

dream. plan. hustle. win.

monthly goals & intentions

family/home

relationships

my body

finances

business

fun/community

personal development I'm committed to

business development I'm committed to

time to reflect

biggest accomplishments
last month?

areas I need to improve
this month?

_____

_____

_____

_____

High Vibe Habit Stacker

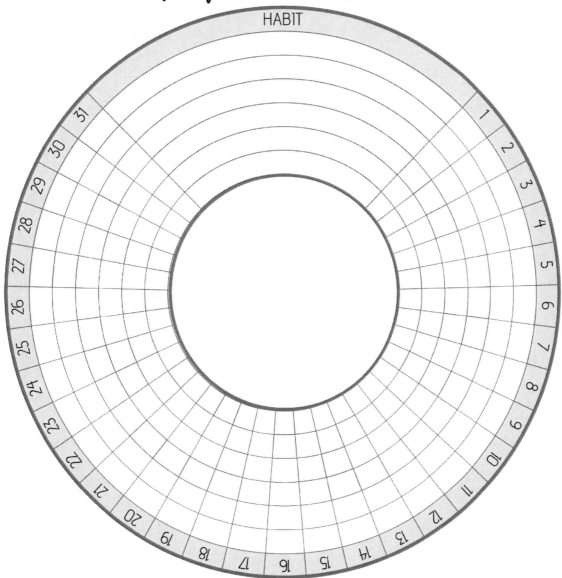

HABIT

Habit Stack	Days Complete	Percentage Complete
		%
		%
		%
		%
		%
		%

Month:

_____

Notes:

_____

_____

_____

_____

_____

_____

_____

_____

_____

sunday	monday	tuesday

wednesday	thursday	friday	saturday

weekly to-do's

- [ ] _____
- [ ] _____
- [ ] _____
- [ ] _____
- [ ] _____
- [ ] _____
- [ ] _____
- [ ] _____
- [ ] _____
- [ ] _____
- [ ] _____
- [ ] _____
- [ ] _____
- [ ] _____
- [ ] _____
- [ ] _____
- [ ] _____

- [ ] _____
- [ ] _____
- [ ] _____
- [ ] _____
- [ ] _____
- [ ] _____
- [ ] _____
- [ ] _____
- [ ] _____
- [ ] _____
- [ ] _____
- [ ] _____
- [ ] _____
- [ ] _____
- [ ] _____
- [ ] _____
- [ ] _____

weekly to-do's

☐ _____
☐ _____
☐ _____
☐ _____
☐ _____
☐ _____
☐ _____
☐ _____
☐ _____
☐ _____
☐ _____
☐ _____
☐ _____
☐ _____
☐ _____
☐ _____
☐ _____

☐ _____
☐ _____
☐ _____
☐ _____
☐ _____
☐ _____
☐ _____
☐ _____
☐ _____
☐ _____
☐ _____
☐ _____
☐ _____
☐ _____
☐ _____
☐ _____
☐ _____

monthly enrollments

Date	Name						

business goals

of new customers

goal _____

actual _____

○ ○ ○ ○ ○
○ ○ ○ ○ ○
○ ○ ○ ○ ○
○ ○ ○ ○ ○

of new team members

goal _____

actual _____

○ ○ ○ ○ ○
○ ○ ○ ○ ○
○ ○ ○ ○ ○
○ ○ ○ ○ ○

of team advancements

goal _____

actual _____

○ ○ ○ ○ ○
○ ○ ○ ○ ○
○ ○ ○ ○ ○
○ ○ ○ ○ ○

of customer invites

goal _____

actual _____

of business opportunity invites

goal _____

actual _____

notes

customer hot list

1.

2.

3.

4.

5.

6.

7.

8.

9.

10.

11.

12.

13.

14.

15.

16.

17.

18.

19.

20.

21.

22.

23.

24.

25.

26.

27.

28.

29.

30.

31.

32.

33.

34.

35.

36.

37.

38.

39.

40.

business hot list

1.

2.

3.

4.

5.

6.

7.

8.

9.

10.

11.

12.

13.

14.

15.

16.

17.

18.

19.

20.

21.

22.

23.

24.

25.

26.

27.

28.

29.

30.

31.

32.

33.

34.

35.

36.

37.

38.

39.

40.

week of: _____

review last week/
plan this week ☐

top three yearly goals
1.
2.
3.

top three monthly goals
1.
2.
3.

top three weekly goals
1.
2.
3.

three most important
meetings/events
1.
2.
3.

	monday		tuesday	
6				
7				
8				
9				
10				
11				
12				
1				
2				
3				
4				
5				
6				
7				
8				
9				
10				
invites	business	customer	business	customer

win the week

Action	Mon	Tues	Weds	Thurs	Fri	Sat	Sun	Goal	Actual	%
Read Vision/Review Goals										
Book of Proof										

wednesday		thursday		friday		saturday		sunday		
										6
										7
										8
										9
										10
										11
										12
										1
										2
										3
										4
										5
										6
										7
										8
										9
										10
business	customer	business	customer	business	customer	business	customer	business	customer	

marketing plan

monday	tuesday	wednesday	thursday	friday	saturday	sunday

remember, life happens for you, not to you.

WINS _____

LOSSES _____

HOW CAN I IMPROVE? _____

week of: _____

review last week/
plan this week ☐

top three yearly goals
1.
2.
3.

top three monthly goals
1.
2.
3.

top three weekly goals
1.
2.
3.

three most important
meetings/events
1.
2.
3.

	monday		tuesday	
6				
7				
8				
9				
10				
11				
12				
1				
2				
3				
4				
5				
6				
7				
8				
9				
10				
invites	business	customer	business	customer

win the week

Action	Mon	Tues	Weds	Thurs	Fri	Sat	Sun	Goal	Actual	%
Read Vision/Review Goals										
Book of Proof										

wednesday		thursday		friday		saturday		sunday		
										6
										7
										8
										9
										10
										11
										12
										1
										2
										3
										4
										5
										6
										7
										8
										9
										10
business	customer	business	customer	business	customer	business	customer	business	customer	

marketing plan

monday	tuesday	wednesday	thursday	friday	saturday	sunday

remember, life happens for you, not to you.

WINS _____

LOSSES _____

HOW CAN I IMPROVE? _____

week of: _____

| review last week/ plan this week | ☐ |

top three yearly goals
1.
2.
3.

top three monthly goals
1.
2.
3.

top three weekly goals
1.
2.
3.

three most important meetings/events
1.
2.
3.

	monday		tuesday	
6				
7				
8				
9				
10				
11				
12				
1				
2				
3				
4				
5				
6				
7				
8				
9				
10				
invites	business	customer	business	customer

win the week

Action	Mon	Tues	Weds	Thurs	Fri	Sat	Sun	Goal	Actual	%
Read Vision/Review Goals										
Book of Proof										

wednesday		thursday		friday		saturday		sunday		
										6
										7
										8
										9
										10
										11
										12
										1
										2
										3
										4
										5
										6
										7
										8
										9
										10
business	customer	business	customer	business	customer	business	customer	business	customer	

marketing plan

monday	tuesday	wednesday	thursday	friday	saturday	sunday

remember, life happens for you, not to you.

WINS _____

LOSSES _____

HOW CAN I IMPROVE? _____

week of: _____

top three yearly goals
1.
2.
3.

top three monthly goals
1.
2.
3.

top three weekly goals
1.
2.
3.

three most important
meetings/events
1.
2.
3.

	monday		tuesday	
6				
7				
8				
9				
10				
11				
12				
1				
2				
3				
4				
5				
6				
7				
8				
9				
10				
invites	business	customer	business	customer

win the week

Action	Mon	Tues	Weds	Thurs	Fri	Sat	Sun	Goal	Actual	%
Read Vision/Review Goals										
Book of Proof										

wednesday		thursday		friday		saturday		sunday		
										6
										7
										8
										9
										10
										11
										12
										1
										2
										3
										4
										5
										6
										7
										8
										9
										10
business	customer	business	customer	business	customer	business	customer	business	customer	

marketing plan

monday	tuesday	wednesday	thursday	friday	saturday	sunday

remember, life happens for you, not to you.

WINS _____

LOSSES _____

HOW CAN I IMPROVE? _____

week of: _____

top three yearly goals
1.
2.
3.

top three monthly goals
1.
2.
3.

top three weekly goals
1.
2.
3.

three most important
meetings/events
1.
2.
3.

	monday		tuesday	
6				
7				
8				
9				
10				
11				
12				
1				
2				
3				
4				
5				
6				
7				
8				
9				
10				
invites	business	customer	business	customer

win the week

Action	Mon	Tues	Weds	Thurs	Fri	Sat	Sun	Goal	Actual	%
Read Vision/Review Goals										
Book of Proof										

wednesday	thursday	friday	saturday	sunday	
					6
					7
					8
					9
					10
					11
					12
					1
					2
					3
					4
					5
					6
					7
					8
					9
					10

business	customer	business	customer	business	customer	business	customer	business	customer

marketing plan

monday	tuesday	wednesday	thursday	friday	saturday	sunday

remember, life happens for you, not to you.

WINS _____

LOSSES _____

HOW CAN I IMPROVE? _____

Month:

dream. plan. hustle. win.

monthly goals & intentions

family/home

relationships

my body

finances

business

fun/community

personal development I'm committed to

business development I'm committed to

time to reflect

biggest accomplishments
last month?

areas I need to improve
this month?

_____

_____

_____

_____

High Vibe Habit Stacker

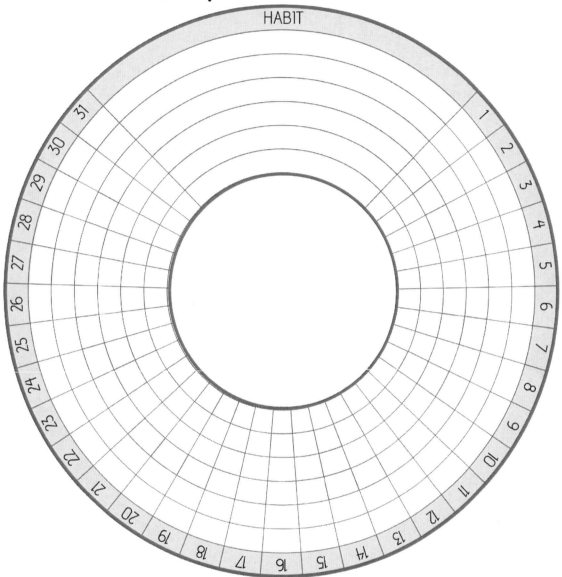

HABIT

Habit Stack	Days Complete	Percentage Complete
		%
		%
		%
		%
		%
		%

Month:

_____

Notes:

_____

_____

_____

_____

_____

_____

_____

_____

_____

_____

_____

sunday	monday	tuesday

wednesday	thursday	friday	saturday

weekly to-do's

☐ _____

☐ _____

☐ _____

☐ _____

☐ _____

☐ _____

☐ _____

☐ _____

☐ _____

☐ _____

☐ _____

☐ _____

☐ _____

☐ _____

☐ _____

☐ _____

☐ _____

☐ _____

☐ _____

☐ _____

weekly to-do's

- [ ] _____
- [ ] _____
- [ ] _____
- [ ] _____
- [ ] _____
- [ ] _____
- [ ] _____
- [ ] _____
- [ ] _____
- [ ] _____
- [ ] _____
- [ ] _____
- [ ] _____
- [ ] _____
- [ ] _____
- [ ] _____
- [ ] _____

- [ ] _____
- [ ] _____
- [ ] _____
- [ ] _____
- [ ] _____
- [ ] _____
- [ ] _____
- [ ] _____
- [ ] _____
- [ ] _____
- [ ] _____
- [ ] _____
- [ ] _____
- [ ] _____
- [ ] _____
- [ ] _____
- [ ] _____

monthly enrollments

Date	Name						

business goals

of new customers

goal _____

actual _____

○ ○ ○ ○ ○
○ ○ ○ ○ ○
○ ○ ○ ○ ○
○ ○ ○ ○ ○

of new team members

goal _____

actual _____

○ ○ ○ ○ ○
○ ○ ○ ○ ○
○ ○ ○ ○ ○
○ ○ ○ ○ ○

of team advancements

goal _____

actual _____

○ ○ ○ ○ ○
○ ○ ○ ○ ○
○ ○ ○ ○ ○
○ ○ ○ ○ ○

of customer invites

goal _____

actual _____

# of business opportunity invites

goal _____

actual _____

notes

customer hot list

1.

2.

3.

4.

5.

6.

7.

8.

9.

10.

11.

12.

13.

14.

15.

16.

17.

18.

19.

20.

21.

22.

23.

24.

25.

26.

27.

28.

29.

30.

31.

32.

33.

34.

35.

36.

37.

38.

39.

40.

business hot list

1.
2.
3.
4.
5.
6.
7.
8.
9.
10.
11.
12.
13.
14.
15.
16.
17.
18.
19.
20.

21.
22.
23.
24.
25.
26.
27.
28.
29.
30.
31.
32.
33.
34.
35.
36.
37.
38.
39.
40.

week of: _____

review last week/
plan this week ☐

top three yearly goals
1.
2.
3.

top three monthly goals
1.
2.
3.

top three weekly goals
1.
2.
3.

three most important
meetings/events
1.
2.
3.

	monday ☐		tuesday ☐	
6				
7				
8				
9				
10				
11				
12				
1				
2				
3				
4				
5				
6				
7				
8				
9				
10				
invites	business	customer	business	customer

win the week

Action	Mon	Tues	Weds	Thurs	Fri	Sat	Sun	Goal	Actual	%
Read Vision/Review Goals										
Book of Proof										

wednesday		thursday		friday		saturday		sunday		
										6
										7
										8
										9
										10
										11
										12
										1
										2
										3
										4
										5
										6
										7
										8
										9
										10
business	customer	business	customer	business	customer	business	customer	business	customer	

marketing plan

monday	tuesday	wednesday	thursday	friday	saturday	sunday

remember, life happens for you, not to you.

WINS _____

LOSSES _____

HOW CAN I IMPROVE? _____

week of: _____

top three yearly goals
1.
2.
3.

top three monthly goals
1.
2.
3.

top three weekly goals
1.
2.
3.

three most important
meetings/events
1.
2.
3.

	monday		tuesday	
6				
7				
8				
9				
10				
11				
12				
1				
2				
3				
4				
5				
6				
7				
8				
9				
10				
invites	business	customer	business	customer

win the week

Action	Mon	Tues	Weds	Thurs	Fri	Sat	Sun	Goal	Actual	%
Read Vision/Review Goals										
Book of Proof										

wednesday		thursday		friday		saturday		sunday		
										6
										7
										8
										9
										10
										11
										12
										1
										2
										3
										4
										5
										6
										7
										8
										9
										10
business	customer	business	customer	business	customer	business	customer	business	customer	

marketing plan

monday	tuesday	wednesday	thursday	friday	saturday	sunday

remember, life happens for you, not to you.

WINS _____

LOSSES _____

HOW CAN I IMPROVE? _____

week of: _____

| review last week/ plan this week ☐ |

top three yearly goals
1.
2.
3.

top three monthly goals
1.
2.
3.

top three weekly goals
1.
2.
3.

three most important
meetings/events
1.
2.
3.

	monday		tuesday	
6				
7				
8				
9				
10				
11				
12				
1				
2				
3				
4				
5				
6				
7				
8				
9				
10				
invites	business	customer	business	customer

win the week

Action	Mon	Tues	Weds	Thurs	Fri	Sat	Sun	Goal	Actual	%
Read Vision/Review Goals										
Book of Proof										

wednesday		thursday		friday		saturday		sunday		
										6
										7
										8
										9
										10
										11
										12
										1
										2
										3
										4
										5
										6
										7
										8
										9
										10
business	customer	business	customer	business	customer	business	customer	business	customer	

marketing plan

monday	tuesday	wednesday	thursday	friday	saturday	sunday

remember, life happens for you, not to you.

WINS _____

LOSSES _____

HOW CAN I IMPROVE? _____

week of: _____

review last week/
plan this week ☐

top three yearly goals
1.
2.
3.

top three monthly goals
1.
2.
3.

top three weekly goals
1.
2.
3.

three most important
meetings/events
1.
2.
3.

	monday		tuesday	
6				
7				
8				
9				
10				
11				
12				
1				
2				
3				
4				
5				
6				
7				
8				
9				
10				
invites	business	customer	business	customer

win the week

Action	Mon	Tues	Weds	Thurs	Fri	Sat	Sun	Goal	Actual	%
Read Vision/Review Goals										
Book of Proof										

wednesday	thursday	friday	saturday	sunday	
					6
					7
					8
					9
					10
					11
					12
					1
					2
					3
					4
					5
					6
					7
					8
					9
					10
business	customer	business	customer	business	customer	business	customer	business	customer

marketing plan

monday	tuesday	wednesday	thursday	friday	saturday	sunday

remember, life happens for you, not to you.

WINS _____

LOSSES _____

HOW CAN I IMPROVE? _____

week of: _____

top three yearly goals
1.
2.
3.

top three monthly goals
1.
2.
3.

top three weekly goals
1.
2.
3.

three most important
meetings/events
1.
2.
3.

	monday ☐		tuesday ☐	
6				
7				
8				
9				
10				
11				
12				
1				
2				
3				
4				
5				
6				
7				
8				
9				
10				
invites	business	customer	business	customer

win the week

Action	Mon	Tues	Weds	Thurs	Fri	Sat	Sun	Goal	Actual	%
Read Vision/Review Goals										
Book of Proof										

wednesday		thursday		friday		saturday		sunday		
										6
										7
										8
										9
										10
										11
										12
										1
										2
										3
										4
										5
										6
										7
										8
										9
										10
business	customer	business	customer	business	customer	business	customer	business	customer	

marketing plan

monday	tuesday	wednesday	thursday	friday	saturday	sunday

remember, life happens for you, not to you.

WINS _____

LOSSES _____

HOW CAN I IMPROVE? _____

Month: _____

dream. plan. hustle. win.

monthly goals & intentions

family/home

relationships

my body

finances

business

fun/community

personal development I'm committed to

business development I'm committed to

time to reflect

biggest accomplishments
last month?

areas I need to improve
this month?

_____

_____

_____

_____

High Vibe Habit Stacker

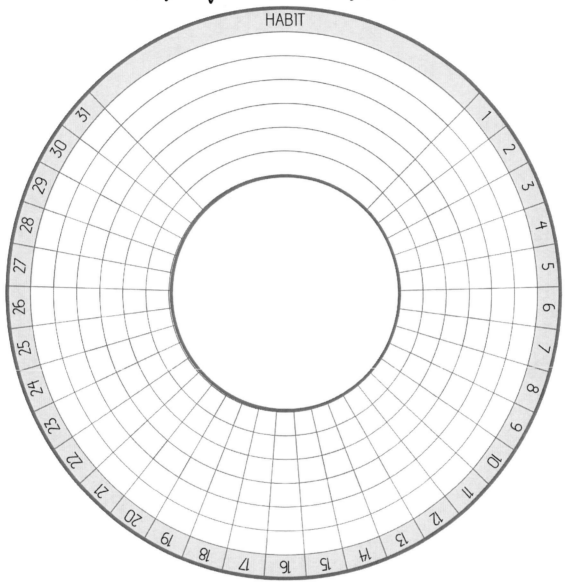

HABIT

Habit Stack	Days Complete	Percentage Complete
		%
		%
		%
		%
		%
		%

Month:

_____

Notes:

_____

_____

_____

_____

_____

_____

_____

_____

_____

_____

sunday	monday	tuesday

wednesday	thursday	friday	saturday

weekly to-do's

- [ ] _____
- [ ] _____
- [ ] _____
- [ ] _____
- [ ] _____
- [ ] _____
- [ ] _____
- [ ] _____
- [ ] _____
- [ ] _____
- [ ] _____
- [ ] _____
- [ ] _____
- [ ] _____
- [ ] _____
- [ ] _____
- [ ] _____

- [ ] _____
- [ ] _____
- [ ] _____
- [ ] _____
- [ ] _____
- [ ] _____
- [ ] _____
- [ ] _____
- [ ] _____
- [ ] _____
- [ ] _____
- [ ] _____
- [ ] _____
- [ ] _____
- [ ] _____
- [ ] _____
- [ ] _____

weekly to-do's

- [ ] _____
- [ ] _____
- [ ] _____
- [ ] _____
- [ ] _____
- [ ] _____
- [ ] _____
- [ ] _____
- [ ] _____
- [ ] _____
- [ ] _____
- [ ] _____
- [ ] _____
- [ ] _____
- [ ] _____
- [ ] _____
- [ ] _____

- [ ] _____
- [ ] _____
- [ ] _____
- [ ] _____
- [ ] _____
- [ ] _____
- [ ] _____
- [ ] _____
- [ ] _____
- [ ] _____
- [ ] _____
- [ ] _____
- [ ] _____
- [ ] _____
- [ ] _____
- [ ] _____
- [ ] _____

monthly enrollments

Date	Name						

business goals

of new customers

goal _____

actual _____

○ ○ ○ ○ ○
○ ○ ○ ○ ○
○ ○ ○ ○ ○
○ ○ ○ ○ ○

of new team members

goal _____

actual _____

○ ○ ○ ○ ○
○ ○ ○ ○ ○
○ ○ ○ ○ ○
○ ○ ○ ○ ○

of team advancements

goal _____

actual _____

○ ○ ○ ○ ○
○ ○ ○ ○ ○
○ ○ ○ ○ ○
○ ○ ○ ○ ○

of customer invites

goal _____

actual _____

of business opportunity invites

goal _____

actual _____

notes

customer hot list

1.
2.
3.
4.
5.
6.
7.
8.
9.
10.
11.
12.
13.
14.
15.
16.
17.
18.
19.
20.

21.
22.
23.
24.
25.
26.
27.
28.
29.
30.
31.
32.
33.
34.
35.
36.
37.
38.
39.
40.

business hot list

1.	21.
2.	22.
3.	23.
4.	24.
5.	25.
6.	26.
7.	27.
8.	28.
9.	29.
10.	30.
11.	31.
12.	32.
13.	33.
14.	34.
15.	35.
16.	36.
17.	37.
18.	38.
19.	39.
20.	40.

week of: _____

**review last week/
plan this week** ☐

top three yearly goals
1.
2.
3.

top three monthly goals
1.
2.
3.

top three weekly goals
1.
2.
3.

three most important
meetings/events
1.
2.
3.

	monday		tuesday	
6				
7				
8				
9				
10				
11				
12				
1				
2				
3				
4				
5				
6				
7				
8				
9				
10				
invites	business	customer	business	customer

win the week

Action	Mon	Tues	Weds	Thurs	Fri	Sat	Sun	Goal	Actual	%
Read Vision/Review Goals										
Book of Proof										

wednesday		thursday		friday		saturday		sunday		
										6
										7
										8
										9
										10
										11
										12
										1
										2
										3
										4
										5
										6
										7
										8
										9
										10
business	customer	business	customer	business	customer	business	customer	business	customer	

marketing plan

monday	tuesday	wednesday	thursday	friday	saturday	sunday

remember, life happens for you, not to you.

WINS _____

LOSSES _____

HOW CAN I IMPROVE? _____

week of: _____

review last week/
plan this week ☐

top three yearly goals
1.
2.
3.

top three monthly goals
1.
2.
3.

top three weekly goals
1.
2.
3.

three most important
meetings/events
1.
2.
3.

	monday		tuesday	
6				
7				
8				
9				
10				
11				
12				
1				
2				
3				
4				
5				
6				
7				
8				
9				
10				
invites	business	customer	business	customer

win the week

Action	Mon	Tues	Weds	Thurs	Fri	Sat	Sun	Goal	Actual	%
Read Vision/Review Goals										
Book of Proof										

wednesday		thursday		friday		saturday		sunday		
										6
										7
										8
										9
										10
										11
										12
										1
										2
										3
										4
										5
										6
										7
										8
										9
										10
business	customer	business	customer	business	customer	business	customer	business	customer	

marketing plan

monday	tuesday	wednesday	thursday	friday	saturday	sunday

remember, life happens for you, not to you.

WINS _____

LOSSES _____

HOW CAN I IMPROVE? _____

week of: _____

**review last week/
plan this week** ☐

top three yearly goals
1.
2.
3.

top three monthly goals
1.
2.
3.

top three weekly goals
1.
2.
3.

three most important
meetings/events
1.
2.
3.

	monday		tuesday	
6				
7				
8				
9				
10				
11				
12				
1				
2				
3				
4				
5				
6				
7				
8				
9				
10				
invites	business	customer	business	customer

win the week

Action	Mon	Tues	Weds	Thurs	Fri	Sat	Sun	Goal	Actual	%
Read Vision/Review Goals										
Book of Proof										

wednesday		thursday		friday		saturday		sunday		
										6
										7
										8
										9
										10
										11
										12
										1
										2
										3
										4
										5
										6
										7
										8
										9
										10
business	customer	business	customer	business	customer	business	customer	business	customer	

marketing plan

monday	tuesday	wednesday	thursday	friday	saturday	sunday

remember, life happens for you, not to you.

WINS _____

LOSSES _____

HOW CAN I IMPROVE? _____

week of: _____

top three yearly goals
1.
2.
3.

top three monthly goals
1.
2.
3.

top three weekly goals
1.
2.
3.

three most important
meetings/events
1.
2.
3.

	monday		tuesday	
6				
7				
8				
9				
10				
11				
12				
1				
2				
3				
4				
5				
6				
7				
8				
9				
10				
invites	business	customer	business	customer

win the week

Action	Mon	Tues	Weds	Thurs	Fri	Sat	Sun	Goal	Actual	%
Read Vision/Review Goals										
Book of Proof										

wednesday		thursday		friday		saturday		sunday		
										6
										7
										8
										9
										10
										11
										12
										1
										2
										3
										4
										5
										6
										7
										8
										9
										10
business	customer	business	customer	business	customer	business	customer	business	customer	

marketing plan

monday	tuesday	wednesday	thursday	friday	saturday	sunday

remember, life happens for you, not to you.

WINS _____

LOSSES _____

HOW CAN I IMPROVE? _____

week of: _____

review last week/
plan this week ☐

top three yearly goals
1.
2.
3.

top three monthly goals
1.
2.
3.

top three weekly goals
1.
2.
3.

three most important
meetings/events
1.
2.
3.

	monday		tuesday	
6				
7				
8				
9				
10				
11				
12				
1				
2				
3				
4				
5				
6				
7				
8				
9				
10				
invites	business	customer	business	customer

win the week

Action	Mon	Tues	Weds	Thurs	Fri	Sat	Sun	Goal	Actual	%
Read Vision/Review Goals										
Book of Proof										

wednesday		thursday		friday		saturday		sunday		
										6
										7
										8
										9
										10
										11
										12
										1
										2
										3
										4
										5
										6
										7
										8
										9
										10
business	customer	business	customer	business	customer	business	customer	business	customer	

marketing plan

monday	tuesday	wednesday	thursday	friday	saturday	sunday

remember, life happens for you, not to you.

WINS _____

LOSSES _____

HOW CAN I IMPROVE? _____

everything
IS **FIGUREOUTABLE.**

MARIE FORLEO

section 2

HUSTLE. WIN.

notes + takeaways

Have you ever read a book, attended a lecture or meeting, or listened to a podcast and you vaguely remember something of importance but you can't remember where or what it was? THIS is home base for every amazing takeaway, lesson, ah-ha, etc. that you come across. By the end, you'll have compiled a whole year of them, all in one magical place! If you find yourself not utilizing this portion of the book, then you aren't reading, listening or attending enough things to shift your mindset to a higher plane. Doing this simple act, daily, will yield you greater rewards than you could have ever imagined! 10-30 minutes a day! Trust me, the new you will thank you later and you'll feel as if you've discovered the holy grail to betterment.

An important note: You can read every book, attend every lecture, and listen to every podcast, but without ACTION, you've wasted your precious time. You have to follow up learning with MASSIVE ACTION. I try to take action IMMEDIATELY. Over thinking will kill you in this business. Action is the secret to success.

top 10 personal development recommendations

Personal development is an important part of getting clarity in your life and your business. Below are my top 10 personal development recommendations to get you started.

1. The Go Giver by Bob Berg
2. Tribe of Mentors by Tim Ferris
3. The Compound Effect by Darren Hardy
4. Miracle Morning by Hal Elrod
5. Go For No Richard Fenton
6. Law of Attraction by Esther and Jerry Hicks
7. Get Over Your Damn Self by Romi Neustadt
8. Think and Grow Rich by Napoleon Hill
9. First Steps to Wealth by Dani Johnson
10. You are a Badass by Jen Sincero

week of: _____

date of call

speaker

takeaways

actions to take

personal development

title of book/podcast/workshop

takeaways

actions to take

week of: _____

speaker

takeaways

actions to take

personal development

title of book/podcast/workshop

takeaways

actions to take

week of: _____

speaker

takeaways

actions to take

personal development

title of book/podcast/workshop

takeaways

actions to take

week of: _____

speaker

takeaways

actions to take

personal development

title of book/podcast/workshop

takeaways

actions to take

week of: _____

speaker

takeaways

actions to take

personal development

title of book/podcast/workshop

takeaways

actions to take

week of: _____

speaker

takeaways

actions to take

personal development

title of book/podcast/workshop

takeaways

actions to take

week of: _____

speaker

takeaways

actions to take

personal development

title of book/podcast/workshop

takeaways

actions to take

week of: _____

speaker

takeaways

actions to take

personal development

title of book/podcast/workshop

takeaways

actions to take

week of: _____

speaker

takeaways

actions to take

title of book/podcast/workshop

takeaways

actions to take

week of: _____

speaker

takeaways

actions to take

personal development

title of book/podcast/workshop

takeaways

actions to take

week of: _____

speaker

takeaways

actions to take

title of book/podcast/workshop

takeaways

actions to take

week of: _____

speaker

takeaways

actions to take

personal development

title of book/podcast/workshop

takeaways

actions to take

week of: _____

speaker

takeaways

actions to take

personal development

title of book/podcast/workshop

takeaways

actions to take

week of: _____

speaker

takeaways

actions to take

personal development

title of book/podcast/workshop

takeaways

actions to take

week of: _____

speaker

takeaways

actions to take

personal development

title of book/podcast/workshop

takeaways

actions to take

week of: _____

speaker

takeaways

actions to take

personal development

title of book/podcast/workshop

takeaways

actions to take

week of: _____

speaker

takeaways

actions to take

personal development

title of book/podcast/workshop

takeaways

actions to take

week of: _____

date of call

speaker

takeaways

actions to take

personal development

title of book/podcast/workshop

takeaways

actions to take

week of: _____

date of call

speaker

takeaways

actions to take

personal development

title of book/podcast/workshop

takeaways

actions to take

week of: _____

speaker

takeaways

actions to take

personal development

title of book/podcast/workshop

takeaways

actions to take

week of: _____

speaker

takeaways

actions to take

personal development

title of book/podcast/workshop

takeaways

actions to take

week of: _____

speaker

takeaways

actions to take

title of book/podcast/workshop

takeaways

actions to take

week of: _____

date of call

speaker

takeaways

actions to take

personal development

title of book/podcast/workshop

takeaways

actions to take

week of: _____

speaker

takeaways

actions to take

personal development

title of book/podcast/workshop

takeaways

actions to take

week of: _____

date of call

speaker

takeaways

actions to take

personal development

title of book/podcast/workshop

takeaways

actions to take

week of: _____

speaker

takeaways

actions to take

personal development

title of book/podcast/workshop

takeaways

actions to take

week of: _____

date of call

speaker

takeaways

actions to take

personal development

title of book/podcast/workshop

takeaways

actions to take

week of: _____

date of call

speaker

takeaways

actions to take

personal development

title of book/podcast/workshop

takeaways

actions to take

week of: _____

date of call

speaker

takeaways

actions to take

personal development

title of book/podcast/workshop

takeaways

actions to take

week of: _____

speaker

takeaways

actions to take

title of book/podcast/workshop

takeaways

actions to take

week of: _____

speaker

takeaways

actions to take

title of book/podcast/workshop

takeaways

actions to take

week of: _____

speaker

takeaways

actions to take

personal development

title of book/podcast/workshop

takeaways

actions to take

week of: _____

date of call

speaker

takeaways

actions to take

personal development

title of book/podcast/workshop

takeaways

actions to take

week of: _____

date of call

speaker

takeaways

actions to take

personal development

title of book/podcast/workshop

takeaways

actions to take

week of: _____

speaker

takeaways

actions to take

personal development

title of book/podcast/workshop

takeaways

actions to take

week of: _____

speaker

takeaways

actions to take

personal development

title of book/podcast/workshop

takeaways

actions to take

week of: _____

date of call

speaker

takeaways

actions to take

personal development

title of book/podcast/workshop

takeaways

actions to take

week of: _____

date of call

speaker

takeaways

actions to take

personal development

title of book/podcast/workshop

takeaways

actions to take

week of: _____

date of call

speaker

takeaways

actions to take

personal development

title of book/podcast/workshop

takeaways

actions to take

week of: _____

date of call

speaker

takeaways

actions to take

personal development

title of book/podcast/workshop

takeaways

actions to take

week of: _____

date of call

speaker

takeaways

actions to take

personal development

title of book/podcast/workshop

takeaways

actions to take

week of: _____

date of call

speaker

takeaways

actions to take

personal development

title of book/podcast/workshop

takeaways

actions to take

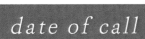

week of: _____

date of call

speaker

takeaways

actions to take

personal development

title of book/podcast/workshop

takeaways

actions to take

week of: _____

speaker

takeaways

actions to take

personal development

title of book/podcast/workshop

takeaways

actions to take

week of: _____

speaker

takeaways

actions to take

personal development

title of book/podcast/workshop

takeaways

actions to take

week of: _____

date of call

speaker

takeaways

actions to take

personal development

title of book/podcast/workshop

takeaways

actions to take

week of: _____

date of call

speaker

takeaways

actions to take

personal development

title of book/podcast/workshop

takeaways

actions to take

week of: _____

date of call

speaker

takeaways

actions to take

personal development

title of book/podcast/workshop

takeaways

actions to take

week of: _____

date of call

speaker

takeaways

actions to take

personal development

title of book/podcast/workshop

takeaways

actions to take

week of: _____

date of call

speaker

takeaways

actions to take

personal development

title of book/podcast/workshop

takeaways

actions to take

week of: _____

date of call

speaker

takeaways

actions to take

personal development

title of book/podcast/workshop

takeaways

actions to take

week of: _____

speaker

takeaways

actions to take

personal development

title of book/podcast/workshop

takeaways

actions to take

week of: _____

date of call

speaker

takeaways

actions to take

personal development

title of book/podcast/workshop

takeaways

actions to take

Made in United States
North Haven, CT
14 April 2023

35455395R00180